STRATEGIC CURRENTS
"TRIGGERED"
AND
"MOBILISED"
Evolving Identities and Implications
for National Cohesion and Security

Strategic Currents

Print ISSN: 3029-1836
Online ISSN: 3029-1828

Series Editors:

Bernard F.W. Loo
S. Rajaratnam School of International Studies
Nanyang Technological University, Singapore

James Char
S. Rajaratnam School of International Studies
Nanyang Technological University, Singapore

Strategic Currents is an annual publication by the S. Rajaratnam School of International Studies. Each issue will be a collection of original essays by prominent scholars in the field of international security, centred on an issue or theme of emerging significance for regional and international security.

Published by World Scientific Publishing Co. Pte. Ltd.:

Strategic Currents: "Triggered" and "Mobilised":
Evolving Identities and Implications for National Cohesion and Security
    edited by Bernard F.W. Loo and Damien D. Cheong

Strategic Currents: China and US Competition for Influence
    edited by Bernard F.W. Loo and James Char

Published by S. Rajaratnam School of International Studies,
Nanyang Technological University and Institute of Southeast Asian Studies,
National University of Singapore:

Strategic Currents: Issues in Human Security in Asia
    edited by Yang Razali Kassim

Strategic Currents: Emerging Trends in Southeast Asia
    edited by Yang Razali Kassim

Published by S. Rajaratnam School of International Studies,
Nanyang Technological University:

Strategic Currents: Marking the Transition to the S. Rajaratnam School of
International Studies
    edited by Yang Razali Kassim

STRATEGIC CURRENTS

"TRIGGERED"
AND
"MOBILISED"

Evolving Identities and Implications
for National Cohesion and Security

Edited by
Bernard F.W. Loo
Damien D. Cheong

Published by

World Scientific Publishing Co. Pte. Ltd.
5 Toh Tuck Link, Singapore 596224
USA office: 27 Warren Street, Suite 401-402, Hackensack, NJ 07601
UK office: 57 Shelton Street, Covent Garden, London WC2H 9HE

National Library Board, Singapore Cataloguing in Publication Data
Name(s): Loo, Bernard Fook Weng, editor. | Cheong, Damien Dominic, editor. | S. Rajaratnam School of International Studies, publisher.
Title: "Triggered" and "mobilised" : evolving identities and implications for national cohesion and security / edited by Bernard F.W. Loo, Damien D. Cheong.
Other Title(s): Strategic currents.
Description: Singapore : S. Rajaratnam School of International Studies : World Scientific Publishing Co. Pte. Ltd., [2025]
Identifier(s): ISBN 978-981-98-1268-4 (hardcover) | 978-981-98-1269-1 (ebook for institutions)) | 978-981-98-1270-7 (ebook for individuals)
Subject(s): LCSH: Internet and activism--Social aspects. | Youth--Political activity--Social aspects.
Classification: DDC 303.484--dc23

British Library Cataloguing-in-Publication Data
A catalogue record for this book is available from the British Library.

Copyright © 2025 by Nanyang Technological University, Singapore

All rights reserved.

For any available supplementary material, please visit
https://www.worldscientific.com/worldscibooks/10.1142/14299#t=suppl

Desk Editors: Kannan Krishnan/Kura Sunaina

Typeset by Stallion Press
Email: enquiries@stallionpress.com

About the Editors

Bernard F. W. Loo is a Senior Fellow and Editor of *Strategic Currents*, S. Rajaratnam School of International Studies (RSIS), Nanyang Technological University (NTU), Singapore. He is concurrently the Coordinator of the Master of Science (Strategic Studies) degree programme. He completed his doctoral studies at the Department of International Politics at the University of Wales, Aberystwyth, in 2002. He is the author of *Medium Powers and Accidental Wars: A Study in Conventional Strategic Stability* (Edwin Mellen, 2005). His edited volume, *Military Transformation and Operations* (Routledge, 2009), was translated into complex Chinese for the Taiwanese military. His other publications have appeared in the *Journal of Strategic Studies, Contemporary Southeast Asia, NIDS Security Reports*, and *Taiwan Defense Affairs*. He is a regular commentator on defence matters, and his commentaries have appeared in *The Straits Times* (Singapore), *The Nation* (Thailand), and *The New Straits Times* (Malaysia).

About the Editors

Damien D. Cheong is Coordinator of the Centre of Excellence for National Security (CENS) and Senior Manager (Horizon Scanning), Executive Deputy Chairman's Office, S. Rajaratnam School of International Studies (RSIS), Nanyang Technological University (NTU), Singapore. He was formerly the Coordinator of the National Security Studies Programme (NSSP), RSIS. Prior to that, he was a Research Fellow and Coordinator of the Homeland Defence Programme at CENS, RSIS, from 2011–2017. He has researched and written on various topics related to national security, strategic communications, and political violence. His current interest is in emerging technologies in relation to national security issues.

About the Contributors

Saddiq Basha is a Research Analyst at the International Centre for Political Violence and Terrorism Research (ICPVTR), a constituent unit of the S. Rajaratnam School of International Studies (RSIS) at Nanyang Technological University (NTU), Singapore. He holds a Bachelor of Social Sciences (Honours) in Political Science from the National University of Singapore (NUS) and is currently pursuing an MSc in Strategic Studies at RSIS, NTU. His research focuses on the digital landscape of far-right extremism, particularly the ideologies, networks, and activities of far-right online communities and subcultures in Southeast Asia and beyond.

Muhammad Haziq Bin Jani is a Senior Analyst at the Indonesia Programme, Institute of Defence and Strategic Studies, S Rajaratnam School of International Studies (RSIS), Nanyang Technological University (NTU), Singapore. Other than the political economy of Indonesia, his research interests include inter-religious relations, Islamism, extremism, and political violence.

Antara Chakraborthy is a Senior Research Analyst at the Centre of Excellence for National Security (CENS) at the S. Rajaratnam School of International Studies (RSIS), Nanyang Technological University (NTU), Singapore. With a background in journalism covering Indian domestic politics, she now explores multiculturalism and citizenship in plural societies. Antara's research focuses on the areas of social cohesion, social resilience, and polarisation in multicultural landscapes. Her current research delves into the rise of religious nationalism in India and its impacts on diasporic identity. Antara loves cats, tea, and a good fantasy novel.

Yasmine Wong is an Associate Research Fellow at the Centre of Excellence for National Security (CENS) at the S. Rajaratnam School of International Studies (RSIS), Nanyang Technological University (NTU), Singapore. Yasmine's research broadly focuses on social resilience, social cohesion, and inter-group relations in online and offline spaces. Her research explores issues surrounding citizenship, race, sexuality, and identity in Singapore, as well as gendered experiences and misogyny in the online sphere. She is co-editor of *Gender and Security in Digital Space: Navigating Access, Harassment, and Disinformation*.

Margareth Sembiring, PhD, is a Research Fellow at the Centre for Non-Traditional Security Studies (NTS Centre), S. Rajaratnam School of International Studies (RSIS), Nanyang Technological University (NTU), Singapore. Her research focuses on environmental and climate change governance, with a strong interest in low-carbon energy transition. She holds a PhD in International Relations from Nanyang Technological University, a Master's degree in International Peace and Security from King's College London as a recipient of the prestigious Chevening Scholarship, a Master's degree in Defence and Security Management from the Indonesian Defence University where she graduated top of her cohort, and a Bachelor's degree in Mechanical Engineering from the National University of Singapore. Her works have been featured in several edited volumes and prominent platforms, including the *Council* on *Foreign Relations*, the *National Bureau of Asian Research*, the *East Asia Forum*, the *Straits Times*, and *the Jakarta Post*. Most recently, she published "Critical Geopolitics of Global Environmental Norms: Exploring Indonesia's Response to Climate Mitigation Agenda" in *Geopolitics Journal*. In addition to her research, Dr Sembiring manages the Secretariat of the NTS-Asia Consortium, a network of research organisations working on NTS issues across the Asia-Pacific region.

Amanda Huan, PhD, is a Research Fellow in the Social Cohesion Research Programme at the S. Rajaratnam School of International Studies (RSIS), Nanyang Technological University (NTU), Singapore. Her broad research interests include international institutions, political psychology, and conflict and peacebuilding. In her work at RSIS, she looks at social cohesion issues and their intersections with contemporary issues such as sustainability, social activism, and digital religion. She possesses a BA in Psychology/Criminology from Adams State College and an undergraduate honours degree in Communication Studies and Psychology from NTU. She completed her MSc and PhD in International Relations at RSIS. Her previous works have been published in journals such as *Armed Forces & Society and Global Change, Peace & Security*. She also co-edited *Faith, Identity, Cohesion: Building a Better Future* (2020).

Jasvir Singh is a prolific community activist and leading figure in the British South Asian community. He has been described by the BBC as "one of the most prominent Sikh voices in British public life". He is a practising family law barrister and a regular contributor to BBC Radio 4's *Thought for the Day*, listened to by 6 million people. He is a trustee and patron of several regional and national charities within the faith and minorities sector, including City Sikhs and the Faiths Forum for London, as well as LGBTQ+ charities such as the Kaleidoscope Trust amongst others. He is the co-founder of South Asian Heritage Month, an annual awareness month which celebrates and commemorates South Asian arts, culture, history, and identity. He was honoured with an OBE in 2017 and a CBE in 2023 for his extensive community work, and he was awarded the "Alumnus of the Year" by King's College London in 2023.

Leong Chan-Hoong, PhD, is a Senior Fellow and Head of the Social Cohesion Research Programme at the S. Rajaratnam School of International Studies (RSIS), Nanyang Technological University (NTU), Singapore. Prior to this, he held senior appointments in various academic institutions, most recently in a global policy advisory firm (Verian Group, formerly Kantar Public). Chan-Hoong sits on the International Advisory Board of the Centre for Applied Cross-cultural Research at Victoria University of Wellington, New Zealand. He is a Fellow and elected board member of the International Academy for Intercultural Research, where he chairs the Rae and Dan Landis Outstanding PhD Dissertation Award Committee. He is a council member at the National Integration Council at the Ministry of Culture, Community, and Youth, and has consulted widely for various government agencies (e.g., defence, education, and population), statutory boards (e.g., People's Association) and international organisations, including the Israel Science Foundation and Konrad Adenauer Stiftung.

© 2025 Nanyang Technological University
https://doi.org/10.1142/9789819812691_fmatter

Contents

About the Editors		v
About the Contributors		vii
Introduction	"Triggered" and "Mobilised": Evolving Identities and Implications for National Cohesion and Security *Bernard F. W. Loo and Damien D. Cheong*	xiii
Part 1	**Far-Right Extremism**	**1**
Chapter 1	The Far-Right and Youth – Global Developments *Damien D. Cheong*	3
Chapter 2	Lurking in the Digital Archipelago: A Case Study of an Online Extreme-Right Community in Southeast Asia *Saddiq Basha*	17
Chapter 3	Far-Right Extremism and Singaporean Youths – Countermeasures and Implications for Decision/Policymakers *Muhammad Haziq Bin Jani*	29
Part 2	**Hindutva**	**39**
Chapter 4	Hindutva's Global Appeal – Recent Developments *Antara Chakraborthy*	41

Chapter 5	Hindutva and Social Cohesion in Singapore *Antara Chakraborthy*	53
Part 3	**Woke Movement**	**65**
Chapter 6	The Implications of the Woke and Anti-Woke Movements on Social Cohesion *Yasmine Wong*	67
Part 4	**Environmental/Climate Activism**	**79**
Chapter 7	Environmental/Climate Activism and Youth: An Update *Margareth Sembiring*	81
Chapter 8	Generation Green: How Young Activists Are Shaping Singapore's Climate Future Part 1 *Amanda Huan*	91
Chapter 9	Generation Green: How Young Activists are Shaping Singapore's Climate Future Part 2 *Amanda Huan*	99
Part 5	**Fostering Social Cohesion**	**109**
Chapter 10	Identity, Youth, and Activism in the Diaspora – The British Sikh Community *Jasvir Singh*	111
Chapter 11	Fostering Social Cohesion by Tackling Shared Challenges as "We" *Amanda Huan and Leong Chan-Hoong*	119

INTRODUCTION

"Triggered" and "Mobilised": Evolving Identities and Implications for National Cohesion and Security

Bernard F. W. Loo and Damien D. Cheong

In November 2023, a 16-year-old Singaporean of Chinese ethnicity was placed under a restriction order under the Internal Security Act; the teenager had been self-radicalised into identifying as a white supremacist by far-right extremist ideologies he had gained access to via online sources.[1] This case was the latest involving far-right extremism in Singapore. For instance, in 2021, another 16-year-old Singaporean was detained under the Internal Security Act for planning to attack and kill worshippers in two mosques on 15 March. He had been motivated by the killing of worshippers in a mosque in Christchurch, New Zealand, by a far-right extremist on 15 March 2019.[2]

The overarching puzzle in both cases is not only the seeming embrace or buy-in of a foreign ideology (i.e., far right) by locals but also the willingness to perpetrate violence because of it. In other words, they were "triggered" and "mobilised". This gave rise to a broader enquiry – what other "foreign" ideologies were out there? Could they potentially trigger and mobilise Singaporeans to act violently? And if so, how might these risks be mitigated? This issue of *Strategic Currents* is a modest attempt to address these questions.

This collection is divided into five parts. The first part discusses the phenomenon of far-right extremism. Contributors Damien D. Cheong, Saddiq Basha, and Haziq Bin Jani discuss far-right extremism in the West and its emergence in Southeast Asia, particularly online as well as implications for Singapore. The second part focuses on Hindutva. Contributor Antara Chakraborthy discusses its appeal and implications for Singapore. The third part explores woke culture. Yasmine Wong discusses its appeal and implications for Singapore. The fourth part examines environmental activism. Margareth Sembiring and Amanda Huan analyse its appeal and implications for Singapore. In the final part, Jasvir Singh writes about the UK experience and provides suggestions on how to better engage Sikh youth. Amanda Huan and Leong Chan-Hoong offer their reflections on how best to mitigate risks to social cohesion.

The editors hope the reader will find these chapters informative and useful.

Endnotes

1. "Self-radicalised S'porean, 16, who identified as white supremacist, given restriction order under ISA", Straits Times, November 8, 2024. https://www.straitstimes.com/singapore/self-radicalised-s-porean-16-who-identified-as-white-supremacist-given-restriction-order-under-isa.
2. "16-year-old Singaporean detained under ISA for planning terrorist attacks on two mosques", Straits Times, January 27, 2021. https://www.straitstimes.com/singapore/16-year-old-detained-under-isa-for-planning-terrorist-attacks-at-two-mosques-in-singapore.

PART 1

FAR-RIGHT EXTREMISM

© 2025 Nanyang Technological University
https://doi.org/10.1142/9789819812691_0001

CHAPTER 1

The Far-Right and Youth – Global Developments

Damien D. Cheong

Key Points
- Over the next three years, youth support for far-right ideals and their possible involvement in extremism is likely.
- This is due to several push factors such as personal/identity issues, the active use of social media and gaming platforms by far-right groups to propagandise and recruit, and dissatisfaction with socio-political and economic conditions.
- A major challenge for policing online activities is that far-right groups and individuals can easily switch and move from one platform to another.
- A multiracial far-right, the far-right's use of AI, and hostile state campaigns in relation to pushing far-right agendas are watch areas.
- AI and other offline strategies can potentially be leveraged to conduct interventions and mitigate risks.

Introduction

Over the next three years, youth support for far-right ideals and their possible involvement in extremism is likely. This is due to several push factors such as personal/identity issues, the active use of emerging technologies by far-right groups to propagandise and recruit, and dissatisfaction with socio-political and economic conditions.

Far-right ideology is not new and has been around for a long time albeit existing at the fringes. It has slowly gathered momentum and become mainstream over the last decade.[1]

Youth support for the far-right appears to be on the rise in many Western countries. In Europe for example, far-right parties like Germany's Alternative for Germany (AfD), France's National Rally, and the European Parliament's Identity and Democracy (ID) have made significant political gains in recent elections due to young voters.[2] In the US, some polls suggest that American youth, especially males, have become more right-leaning and favour "Republican control of Congress".[3]

Far-right extremism[4] involving young people has also become a serious challenge. In 2024, many youths actively participated in the UK riots,[5] which were instigated by far-right provocateurs.[6] In Türkiye, an 18-year-old, suspected to have been influenced by far-right extremism, carried out and live-streamed a stabbing attack.[7] In France, authorities arrested an 18-year-old neo-Nazi for allegedly planning attacks on the Paris Olympics.[8] In 2023, an 18-year-old with extreme far-right tendencies was arrested in Germany on suspicion of planning an attack.[9]

Various Factors Make Far-Right Ideology and its Extremism Appealing to Youth

An individual's embrace of far-right ideology and extremism varies;[10] there can be many push–pull factors.[11] Nevertheless, experts have identified several factors that generally explain this phenomenon: (a) personal/identity issues; (b) online activities of far-right individuals/groups; and (c) broader social, political, and economic issues.

1. Personal/Identity Issues

According to some researchers, young people who are experiencing personal and/or identity issues can be more susceptible to far-right ideology.[12] This is because they are still developing their identities, trying to make sense of the world,[13] and seeking purpose/belonging. Far-right ideologues and groups offer solutions. They provide black-and-white answers/explanations (e.g., like who to blame for problems), convince young people that they will be contributing to a noble cause, and give them a sense of purpose, structure, belonging, and recognition.[14]

A novel approach used by far-right groups is to organise active clubs, where young people train "in sport or physical combat" to form fraternities.[15] Such active clubs have sprung up in Australia, Europe, and the US. "By presenting a more palatable image to the public and combining its extremist ideology with exercise, fitness and MMA training, Active Clubs have widened their appeal to reach a much broader audience than traditional white supremacist groups whose members are often derided for being 'keyboard warriors'".[16]

2. Online activities of far-right individuals/groups

As young people are digital natives, far-right personalities and groups expectedly leverage social media including encrypted messaging apps to connect with, radicalise, and recruit the young.[17]

Far-right online activities have been enhanced by two main enablers. The first is the emergence of charismatic, social media-savvy personalities or influencers who make far-right ideologies and agendas more appealing to younger audiences.[18] Such personalities include American Paul Nicholas Miller, who "advocates for a race war, and espouses white supremacist and neo-Nazi rhetoric"[19] and the UK's Tommy Robinson (aka Stephen Yaxley-Lennon), who propagates Islamophobic rhetoric and is accused of spreading misinformation to stir anti-immigrant sentiment.[20]

The second is social media algorithms that are "designed for engagement ... [but] ... inadvertently create echo chambers ... [that] ... reinforce extreme ideologies, normalise violence, and increase the risk of radicalisation by isolating individuals from diverse perspectives".[21] While main stream social media companies have become more effective in content moderation, taking down blatant extremist and illegal content or borderline content (i.e., "legal yet harmful") is more difficult to police.[22] Furthermore, the use of encrypted and (closed) chat groups and/or forums enables young people to share, follow, and subscribe to far-right channels.[23]

Relatedly, gaming and gaming platforms (e.g., Stream and Discord) are also being used by far-right groups to connect, share content, form communities, and recruit the young.[24] Steam, for instance, has become a hub for far-right extremism due to its lax content moderation policies, which inevitably allow extremist groups to spread propaganda easily.[25]

In terms of recruitment, far-right groups have been using online platforms popular with youth like Instagram and TikTok to recruit. The UK advocacy group Hope Not Hate (HNH) has observed that UK far-right groups like The British Hand, the National Partisan Movement, and the New British Union have been using Instagram to recruit young people.[26] A recent report by the Institute for Strategic Dialogue highlights that "several real-world fascist or far-right organisations were found openly recruiting on the [TikTok] platform".[27]

A major challenge for policing online activities is that far-right groups and individuals can easily switch and move from one platform to another (e.g., from open to closed) if their activities are discovered and their accounts taken down and/or suspended.[28]

3. Socio-political and economic factors

One major factor explaining the far-right's appeal is the disillusionment and dissatisfaction of the young with current socio-political and economic circumstances. As far-right groups offer different perspectives and solutions to these conditions,[29] they are perceived favourably by the young.

For instance, in Italy, "there is a perception that you can't increase the amount of public spending because debt is high and the EU limits how much debt … [the country] … can hold. So, the [far-right] solution of limiting access to public services by excluding immigrants becomes more appealing to many voters. That helps explain why weak public service provision can lead to higher support for the far-right and heighten concern about immigration".[30] In Germany, the young, anxious over inflation, the economy, and poverty in old age, are more amenable to vote for the far-right AfD.[31] A 2022 Australian study on the far-right and youth found that "For the young men in our sample, the majority of whom were employed in what were once called 'blue-collar' labour sectors, the data suggest that they feel left behind and let down by a range of economic and social changes. They resent work precarity and financial struggle but are encouraged by their peers offline and online to blame feminism, culture wars, gender diversity, political correctness, and so on".[32]

A Multiracial Far-Right, the Far-Right's Use of AI, and Hostile State Campaigns are Watch Areas
A multiracial far-right

The embrace of far-right ideology and extremism by non-whites (aka the "multiracial far-right") is something we should be monitoring.[33] Apart from the involvement of two teens in Singapore in far-right plots, examples from the US, such as Mauricio Garcia, a Latino Neo-Nazi sympathiser who killed eight people in a shooting attack in 2023,[34] and Sai Varshith Kandula, an Indian national with Nazi tendencies who rammed his vehicle into barriers near the White House in 2023,[35] suggest that multiracial far-right extremism can have violent outcomes.

Explanations of this phenomenon in the US and other countries include the following: (a) "benefits by virtue of their proximity to the privileges and power that come with whiteness",[36] (b) a "shared antipathy" for (other) minority groups, e.g., immigrants[37] (of the same ethnicity), blacks, LGBTQ, and women; (c) mainstreaming of hate, cultural superiority, and intolerance; and (d) a desire for dominance.[38]

The far-right's use of AI

Some researchers think that far-right extremist groups' use of AI is still in its infancy.[39] However, as AI technology is developing rapidly, such groups will likely master and exploit it in the foreseeable future. They can potentially use AI to "create massive disinformation campaigns (e.g., deepfake images), feed radicalising pieces of propaganda to unsuspecting online users, gather information on potential targets, or even find instructions to create explosive devices. It can also be exploited to write malware, enabling extremists to attack online infrastructures".[40]

Several far-right groups on Telegram are "dedicated to creating and disseminating AI-generated memes and propaganda".[41] In the UK, far-right groups have used AI to create material such as inflammatory images as well as songs/music to instigate and inflame.[42]

Other possible uses of AI include the following:[43] (a) using AI-backed bots to launch "coordinated" campaigns to produce identical messages to flood social media sites simultaneously, thereby increasing "the scale and engagement of extremist propaganda"; (b) translation of content to help extremists spread their message globally; and (c) evading moderation/detection via AI-translated content.

Hostile state campaigns

The propagation of far-right ideology and extremism can also be part of a hostile state campaign designed to undermine social cohesion and foment dissent. For example, an American media company allegedly funded by Russia, was found to have paid right-wing influencers to push narratives favourable to the Kremlin.[44] In Europe, Russia has been accused of supporting far-right parties as they "are seen [by Moscow] as allies because they in general are seen as centrifugal forces which can erode cohesion in the EU, making it easier for Russia to establish its own hegemony".[45] As all countries have social cleavages, there is always a possibility for exploitation by other countries.

AI Can Potentially Be Used to Mitigate Far-Right Appeal and Extremism

Countering far-right appeal and extremism has been addressed by other authors in this book and will not be discussed here. Instead, the focus will be on how to better leverage AI to conduct interventions and mitigate risks.

According to one researcher, tech companies can do the following:[46] (a) "implement AI-driven content moderation tools to detect and remove extremist propaganda in real-time"; (b) prevent the creation of extremist deepfake images by "identifying and restricting specific word combinations"; and (c) "develop algorithms to identify and flag potentially radicalising content". For such methods to be effective, collaboration between counterterrorism experts, psychologists, tech companies, governments, and NGOs is suggested.

The researcher also suggests using AI tools to do the following:[47] (a) "assess vulnerability to radicalisation by targeting users on video-sharing sites and redirecting them to counter-narrative content" and (b) generate counter-deepfake images to undermine "their leaders or ideologies" to create cognitive dissonance.

Conclusion

The far-right and its extremism are no longer exclusively "white" issues and can emerge in multiracial/multireligious societies and countries. Apart from potentially leveraging emerging technologies to mitigate risks, offline approaches such as those discussed in subsequent chapters of this book can help.

Endnotes

1. J. Ebner, "From margins to mainstream: How extremism has conquered the political middle", *International Centre for Counter-Terrorism (ICCT) Analysis*, August 10, 2023. https://www.icct.nl/publication/margins-mainstream-how-extremism-has-conquered-political-middle; H. Ashby, "Far-right extremism is a global problem", *Foreign Policy*, January 15, 2021. https://foreignpolicy.com/2021/01/15/far-right-extremism-global-problem-worldwide-solutions/.
2. "Why is the far right gaining popularity among young people?" *Euro News*, June 21, 2024. https://www.euronews.com/my-europe/2024/06/21/why-is-the-far-right-gaining-popularity-among-young-people; "It's not just boomers, young people are voting far right too", *Politico*, May 29, 2024. https://www.politico.eu/article/europe-young-people-right-wing-voters-far-right-politics-eu-elections-parliament/.
3. "Young men in the US used to lean left. Could they now hand Trump the presidency?" *The Guardian*, August 5, 2024. https://www.theguardian.com/us-news/ng-interactive/2024/aug/05/young-men-voters-us-election-trump-harris.
4. Far-right extremism (FRE) "does not have a clearly defined ideology, its adherents typically espouse rhetoric championing white (or ethnic) supremacy, xenophobia, racism, ultranationalism, Islamophobia and anti-immigration. Though FRE is often conflated with white supremacy, its broader messages of ethno-religious chauvinism, nationalism, and nativism have found resonance amongst various ethnicities." See Internal Security Department, *Singapore Terrorism Threat Assessment Report 2024*, p. 12. https://www.mha.gov.sg/docs/default-source/default-document-library/sttar-2024.pdf.
5. A 12-year-old boy was charged for public disorder as he had been "part of a crowd of hundreds of rioters who set a police van on fire and tried to storm the Southport Islamic Society Mosque". See "12-year-old boy youngest to be sentenced over UK riots", *AP*, September 18, 2024. https://apnews.com/article/uk-riots-12-year-old-boy-sentenced-b0f3125d2344432aa3ca7426aca7b5d8.
6. The riots were fuelled by far-right extremists capitalising on misinformation that a knife attack that resulted in three fatalities was carried out by a Muslim asylum seeker. See "Explainer: What sparked the far-right riots in the UK and what is the way forward?" *TODAY*, August 8, 2024. https://www.todayonline.com/news/explainer-what-sparked-far-right-riots-uk-and-what-way-forward-2471991.
7. "Turkey arrests teenager for stabbing attack at mosque", *Al-Jazeera*, August 13, 2024. https://www.aljazeera.com/news/2024/8/13/turkey-arrests-teenager-for-stabbing-attack-at-mosque.
8. "French security services arrest far-right extremist over suspected Paris Olympics plot", *France 24*, July 17, 2024. https://www.france24.com/en/france/20240717-french-security-services-arrest-far-right-extremist-suspected-paris-olympics-plot-france.

9. "German police arrest 18-year-old over far-right attack plot", *DW*, November 20, 2023. https://www.dw.com/en/german-police-arrest-18-year-old-over-far-right-attack-plot/a-67500577.
10. P. Nilan, "Young People and the Far Right", *Social Science Matters* (Palgrave Macmillan website). https://www.palgrave.com/gp/blogs/social-sciences/nilan.
11. L. Khalil, "Inquiry into right wing extremist movements in Australia", *Submission to the Legal and Constitutional Affairs References Committee of the Senate*, April 2024. https://www.aph.gov.au/DocumentStore.ashx?id=ff959b90-a30c-4257-98f2-76e4a8e9d9ab&subId=755135.
12. C. M. Idriss, "Youth and the radical right", in J. Rydgren (ed.), *The Oxford Handbook of the Radical Right*, (New York: Oxford University Press, 2018) pp. 348–365; K. Ramakrishna, "CO24016 | Understanding Singapore's 'multicultural white supremacists'", *RSIS Commentary*, January 29, 2024. https://www.rsis.edu.sg/rsis-publication/rsis/understanding-singapores-multicultural-white-supremacists/.
13. N. Malik, "Here's why young people are particularly vulnerable to radicalization", *Forbes*, January 13, 2020. https://www.forbes.com/sites/nikitamalik/2020/01/12/heres-why-young-people-are-vulnerable-radicalization/.
14. P. Nilan. *Op. cit.*
15. "Active Clubs and white supremacy groups targeting young men a 'threat to social cohesion' in Australia", *ABC News*, August 3, 2024. https://www.abc.net.au/news/2024-08-03/active-clubs-white-supremecy-groups-targeting-men/104164174.
16. "Active Clubs: A new far-right threat to democratic elections", *Al-Jazeera*, May 2, 2024. https://www.aljazeera.com/opinions/2024/5/2/active-clubs-a-new-far-right-threat-to-democratic-elections.
17. In Australia, security agencies have warned that the number of young people becoming radicalised by far-right extremist ideologies online has been growing. See "Young Australians are being 'aggressively radicalised' through right-wing extremism, federal police warn", *SBS News*, October 20, 2020. https://www.sbs.com.au/news/article/young-australians-are-being-aggressively-radicalised-through-right-wing-extremism-federal-police-warn/ix5jgqkkc; "ASIO chief flags alarming increase in children lured to extremism", *The Strategist*, February 11, 2022. https://www.aspistrategist.org.au/asio-chief-flags-alarming-increase-in-children-lured-to-extremism/; "Far-right extremism is rising and coming from varied communities, inquiry hears", *SBS News*, June 20, 2024. https://www.sbs.com.au/news/article/far-right-extremism-is-rising-and-coming-from-varied-communities-inquiry-hears/8vhbw5o6k.
18. See "Europe's far right uses TikTok to win youth vote", *Politico*, March 17, 2024. https://www.politico.eu/article/tiktok-far-right-european-parliament-politics-europe/.
19. Internal Security Department. *Op. cit.*, p. 14.
20. "Who is Tommy Robinson, Britain's far-right Islamophobic influencer?" *Le Monde*, August 13, 2024. https://www.lemonde.fr/en/m-le-mag/article/2024/08/13/who-is-tommy-robinson-britain-s-far-right-islamophobic-influencer_6714596_117.html;

"The far right has moved online, where its voice is more dangerous than ever", *The Guardian*, August 3, 2024. https://www.theguardian.com/politics/article/2024/aug/03/the-far-right-has-moved-online-where-its-voice-is-more-dangerous-than-ever.
21. "Extremist groups rely on social media, rooting them out won't be easy", *Forbes*, May 13, 2024. https://www.forbes.com/sites/petersuciu/2024/05/13/extremist-groups-rely-on-social-media-rooting-them-out-wont-be-easy/.
22. The Verwey-Jonker Institute, *Right-wing extremist radicalisation on social media platforms?* August 2023. https://repository.wodc.nl/bitstream/handle/20.500.12832/3304/3341-rechtsextremisme-op-sociale-media-platforms-summary.pdf.
23. *Ibid.*
24. G. Wells, A. Romhanyi, J. G. Reitman, R. Gardner, K. Squire, and C. Steinkuehler, "Right-wing extremism in mainstream games: A review of the literature", *Games and Culture*, 19(4), (2023). https://journals.sagepub.com/doi/10.1177/15554120231167214.
25. S. Shaikh, "Gaining steam: Far-right radicalisation on gaming platforms", *Global Network on Extremism and Technology Insights*, July 29, 2024. https://gnet-research.org/2024/07/29/gaining-steam-far-right-radicalisation-on-gaming-platforms/.
26. "Neo-Nazi groups use Instagram to recruit young people, warns Hope Not Hate", *The Guardian*, Mar 22, 2021. https://www.theguardian.com/world/2021/mar/22/neo-nazi-groups-use-instagram-to-recruit-young-people-warns-hope-not-hate; Hope Not Hate, *State of Hate 2024: Pessimism, Decline and The Rising Radical Right*, p. 127. https://hopenothate.org.uk/wp-content/uploads/2024/03/state-of-hate-2024-v15.pdf.
27. N. Doctor, G. Fiennes, and C. O'Connor, "NazTok: An organized neo-Nazi TikTok network is getting millions of views", *Institute for Strategic Dialogue*, July 29, 2024. https://www.isdglobal.org/digital_dispatches/naztok-an-organized-neo-nazi-tiktok-network-is-getting-millions-of-views/.
28. G. Tan, "How Discord, Steam and other gaming platforms became dominated by the far right", *Straits Times*, January 30, 2024. https://www.straitstimes.com/opinion/how-discord-steam-and-other-gaming-platforms-became-dominated-by-the-far-right.
29. "Terrorism: Police concern over teen far-right extremism", *BBC*, January 26, 2023. https://www.bbc.com/news/uk-wales-64399335.
30. "What the rise of far-right politics says about the economy in an election year", *Harvard Business School Working Knowledge*, May 21, 2024. https://hbswk.hbs.edu/item/what-the-rise-of-far-right-politics-says-about-the-economy-in-an-election-year.
31. "Pessimistic young Germans turning to far right, says study", *DW*, April 23, 2024. https://www.dw.com/en/pessimistic-young-germans-turning-to-far-right-says-study/a-68897441.
32. P. Nilan, J. Roose, M. Peucker, and B. S. Turner, "Young masculinities and right-wing populism in Australia", *Youth*, 3(1), 285–299, February 2023. https://www.mdpi.com/2673-995X/3/1/19.

33. *SBS News. Op. cit.*
34. "What we know about the slain Texas mall massacre suspect, Mauricio Garcia", *NBC News*, May 8, 2023. https://www.nbcnews.com/news/us-news/mauricio-garcia-allen-texas-mall-shooting-suspect-what-know-rcna83242.
35. "Nazi flag-bearing man who crashed a truck into barriers near the White House pleads guilty to felony", *Associated Press*, May 14, 2024. https://apnews.com/article/sai-varshith-kandula-white-house-truck-crash-88971b56fdfb93af0e2c984cd724a441.
36. "Why 'white' supremacists are not always white", *Al Jazeera*, June 2, 2023. https://www.aljazeera.com/opinions/2023/6/2/why-white-supremacists-are-not-always-white.
37. "A far-right Turkish nationalist group known as the Ataman Brotherhood, has been known to commit hate crimes and violence against migrants and refugees" (in Türkiye). See "Far-right extremism is also a growing problem throughout the global south", *Soufan Centre Intelbrief*, August 30, 2024. https://thesoufancenter.org/intelbrief-2024-august-30/.
38. "The allure of fascism: why do minorities join the far right?" *The Guardian*, May 22, 2023. https://www.theguardian.com/world/2023/may/22/minorities-extreme-right-wing-groups-ideology.
39. W. Allchorn, "Global far-right extremist exploitation of artificial intelligence and alt-tech: The cases of the UK, US, Australia and New Zealand", *Counter Terrorist Trends and Analyses (CTTA)*, 16(03), June 12, 2024. https://www.rsis.edu.sg/ctta-newsarticle/global-far-right-extremist-exploitation-of-artificial-intelligence-and-alt-tech-the-cases-of-the-uk-us-australia-and-new-zealand/.
40. F. Borgonovo, S. R. Lucini, and G. Porrino, "Weapons of mass hate dissemination: The use of artificial intelligence by right-wing extremists", *Global Network on Extremism and Technology (GNET) Insights*, February 23, 2024. https://gnet-research.org/2024/02/23/weapons-of-mass-hate-dissemination-the-use-of-artificial-intelligence-by-right-wing-extremists/#.
41. *Ibid.*; See also "Neo-Nazis and white supremacists globally look to artificial intelligence to promote their message, spread misinformation, and aide their cause, January 2023-May 2024", *MEMRI*, June 20, 2024. https://www.memri.org/dttm/neo-nazis-and-white-supremacists-globally-look-artificial-intelligence-promote-their-message-0.
42. "How TikTok bots and AI have powered a resurgence in UK far-right violence", *The Guardian*, August 2, 2024. https://www.theguardian.com/politics/article/2024/aug/02/how-tiktok-bots-and-ai-have-powered-a-resurgence-in-uk-far-right-violence.
43. "AI will amplify terror threat and is already fuelling tensions, say police", *INews*, January 2, 2024. https://inews.co.uk/news/ai-terror-threat-police-already-fuelling-tensions-2825617.

44. "U.S. says Russia funded media company that paid right-wing influencers millions for videos", *CBS News*, September 5, 2024. https://www.cbsnews.com/news/russia-tenet-media-right-wing-influencers-justice-department/.
45. "'Pragmatic manipulation': Is Russia playing with European voters' minds?" *Al Jazeera*, June 5, 2024. https://www.aljazeera.com/features/2024/6/5/pragmatic-manipulation-is-russia-playing-with-european-voters-minds; K. Rekawek, T. Renard, and B. Molas (eds.). *Russia and the Far-Right: Insights from Ten European Countries* (The Hague: ICCT Press, 2024). https://www.icct.nl/sites/default/files/2024-04/Russia%20and%20the%20Far-Right%20Insights%20from%20Ten%20European%20Countries%20-%20A4%20e-book_0.pdf.
46. "The digital weaponry of radicalisation: AI and the recruitment nexus", *Global Network on Extremism and Technology (GNET) Insights*, July 4, 2024. https://gnet-research.org/2024/07/04/the-digital-weaponry-of-radicalisation-ai-and-the-recruitment-nexus/.
47. *Ibid.*

© 2025 Nanyang Technological University
https://doi.org/10.1142/9789819812691_0002

CHAPTER 2

Lurking in the Digital Archipelago: A Case Study of an Online Extreme-Right Community in Southeast Asia

Saddiq Basha

Key Points

- An Austronesian supremacist community exists online, seeking to promote the ethnic superiority of Austronesians.
- The groups/individuals, influenced by the Western Extreme Right, legitimise hate and violence through memes tailored for a Southeast Asian audience.
- The groups/individuals also amalgamate distinct extremist ideologies to expand their reach.
- The groups/individuals reinforce a sense of shared belonging and camaraderie over the creation and consumption of memes.
- The extreme-right online community in Southeast Asia may not currently be in a violent phase; however, this does not preclude the possibility of future violence.

Introduction

In recent years, scholars and practitioners in the Preventing and Countering Violent Extremism (PCVE) field have increasingly recognised that Southeast Asia's (SEA) threat landscape is far from monolithic. This has prompted an expansion of their focus beyond the traditional emphasis on Islamist extremism to encompass the creeping influence and threat posed by extreme-right movements[1] or strands of their ideologies. This shift has come amidst various real-world regional manifestations of extreme-right ideologies. This includes incidents such as the online hate speech- and disinformation-driven xenophobic attacks on Rohingya refugees in Indonesia,[2] the ethno-religious "us-versus-them" narratives that underpinned Malaysia's "Allah" socks controversy that witnessed several arson attacks,[3] and the recent detention of a 16-year-old Chinese Singaporean youth who identified as a white supremacist and planned to carry out attacks abroad.[4]

A common thread among these examples is the crucial role of the digital sphere and embedded online communities in facilitating the dissemination of extremist ideas and rhetoric. That SEA is home to various extreme-right online communities may come as a surprise to some. Regional scholars such as Munira Mustaffa have emphasised the growing influence of these online communities, which range from "politically conservative nationalist actors" to supporters of "pan-Asian movements", often espousing ethno-religious aspirations to establish a "pure" homeland.[5]

One such community that has gained prominence on social media platforms is the Austronesian supremacist community. This community, consisting of a loose network of online users, seeks to promote the ethnic superiority of Austronesians – an ethno-linguistic group with large populations in Maritime Southeast Asia (primarily Indonesia,

Malaysia, and the Philippines). While not organised or violent in the traditional sense, this community actively produces and propagates extreme-right online content in the form of memes reminiscent of those in the Western extreme right's online meme subcultures, though often adapted with a unique SEA twist.[6]

This chapter seeks to provide insights into the Austronesian supremacist online community – specifically by examining its attempts to normalise extremist beliefs and promote violence through memes – its various influences, and its community-building efforts. Some key implications for analysts and policymakers are then discussed.

Influences from the Western Extreme Right: Legitimising Hate and Violence Through Memes

The Western extreme right's widespread use of memes has been recognised by scholars as a key strategic tool in online communication, propaganda, and recruitment. Specifically, they highlight how the extreme right, under the guise of "harmless" irony and humour, produces and shares memes that often simplify and conceal complex extremist ideological narratives.[7] Such narratives often rely on racist and dehumanising imagery, themes of racial superiority and impurity, and the perceived threat of the "Other" (e.g., racial, religious, or sexual minorities).[8] Such seemingly innocuous borderline-radical content, however, risks mainstreaming extremist ideologies and narratives by making them more palatable to a broader (and often younger) audience.[9]

Given the hyperconnectivity of the digital sphere, it is unsurprising that the visual aesthetic and functionality of memes from the Western extreme-right online meme subculture are being adopted and adapted into SEA. This is particularly evident within the Austronesian supremacist online community, where users – observably young men[10] – have been seen incorporating Western extreme-right figures and symbols into their memes and online profiles. Notable examples include the use of Nazi propagandist Joseph Goebbels in memes to convey nativist and xenophobic messages, as well as the inclusion of neo-Nazi symbols, such as the SS lightning bolts and the *Sonnenrad* (black sun), in memes or social media bios to signal ideological affiliations.[11] Other memes found included contemporary references that valorise the violence committed by recent white supremacist mass shooters such as Payton Gendron.[12]

Adapting Memes for Regional Audiences

While the influence of the Western extreme-right online meme subcultures on the Austronesian supremacist community is evident, researchers have noted that the latter actively adapts these influences to align with the local context.[13] This adaptation reflects the fluidity of memes – visual elements are remixed to resonate with local popular culture aesthetics and narratives are adjusted to address perceived regional socio-political issues. For instance, the neo-Nazi *Sonnenrad* symbol is often replaced with the locally relevant *Surya Majapahit* (Majapahit sun) emblem, and regional historical figures such as Filipino nationalist and pan-Malayan advocate Jose Rizal are appropriated to justify ethnic supremacist beliefs.[14]

This process of localisation extends to the extremist narratives embedded within memes. Employing the "Great Replacement" conspiracy theory[15] common in Western extreme-right communities, the Austronesian supremacist community redirects its animosity and calls for violence towards local Rohingya refugees and ethnic minority communities such as the Chinese, whom they perceive as replacing indigenous populations.[16]

It is worth noting that while these memes primarily circulate within the online echo chambers of the Austronesian supremacist community, their localised and borderline-radical nature allows them to occasionally infiltrate the mainstream and gain wider attention. Memes demonising and inciting violence against Rohingya refugees, for instance, have on several occasions gone viral on social media.[17]

Ideological Diversity and Hybridisation within the Austronesian Supremacist Community

Paralleling the diversity of Maritime Southeast Asia, the Austronesian supremacist online community exhibits a range of conceptions of Austronesian supremacy, shaped by its adherence to a unique amalgamation of distinct extremist ideologies. Beyond the predominant nativist, ethno-nationalist strand of this community, there appear to be several subgroups that merge elements of the extreme right with other forms of extremism.

For instance, one subgroup with predominantly Indonesian and Malaysian users draws influences from the visuals, narratives, and ideologies of both the extreme right and Islamist extremism. They call for "Total Rohingya Deaths", incorporating neo-Nazi symbols and slogans while simultaneously using visuals from Islamic State content and celebrating extremist Islamist perpetrators such as Dzhokhar Tsarnaev, one of the Boston Marathon bombers.[18] Such hybridisation between the extreme right and Islamist extremism, according to Alexander Meleagrou-Hitchens and Moustafa Ayad, is neither "random [n]or incoherent".[19] Both movements often overlap since they share similar "reactionary and virulent anti-liberal politics", with a common interest in dismantling liberalism.[20]

However, such hybridisation does not stop with Islamist extremism. Another Austronesian supremacist subgroup, consisting predominantly of Filipino users, subscribes to Falangism, an ideology that emerged in Spain in the 1930s.[21] This fascist ideology combines extreme nationalism, anti-communism, and a return to a strong, traditional national identity, often with a religious component (in this case, Catholicism). On social media, users from this community frequently lament the transformation of the world into a godless society, corrupted by the ills of neo-liberalism, communism, and freemasonry, among others. They co-opt Catholic and Falangist symbols in their content while also adopting extreme-right visual symbols, such as selfies featuring the trademark skull mask of the accelerationist neo-Nazi organisation Atomwaffen Division and making the Nazi salute.

Constructing an Extremist Community: Bridging the Online and Offline Sphere

Despite the lack of an organisational structure, extreme-right online communities such as the Austronesian supremacists can still effectively facilitate the sharing and reinforcement of extremist beliefs. Scholars such as Ana-Maria Biluc explain that such online communities serve as "havens of validation and support for extremist".[22] Put differently, they not only coalesce like-minded individuals but also reinforce the group's values, beliefs, and norms – including ones that may sanction certain violent behaviours to achieve the group's collective goals.[23]

One critical way the Austronesian supremacist online community reinforces a sense of shared belonging and group cohesiveness is through camaraderie forged over the creation and consumption of memes. Mastery of memes and the surrounding subculture serves as a means of communicating one's belonging to the in-group while distancing from the out-group.[24] This can take the form of voicing support in the comment section, where users reaffirm and echo extremist narratives, or through circulating and remixing the memes of others.

Other users, however, go beyond content creation and circulation by actively contributing to community building. They create online groups and channels on encrypted platforms, aiming to coalesce like-minded individuals into spaces where extreme and violent narratives can be more overtly expressed. For instance, one group from the Falangist community actively seeks to recruit users on main platforms like TikTok through videos that call for aspiring "Christo-Fascists" based in the Philippines to join their server on the gaming-adjacent platform Discord.[25]

In this private space, the group moderator shares various reading materials, such as antisemitic books like "The Myth of German Villainy", videos promoting Judeo-Masonic conspiracy theories, and posters blaming democracy and liberalism for the world's ills. Communication, however, is not one-sided. Various users can be observed engaging in conversations and debates, including rather eschatological arguments that "the Philippines is a hope for the West", being one of the last bastions of Catholicism.

Interestingly, their activities extend beyond the digital realm into real-life activism. For example, the group has held several events, such as "Activism through Action", encouraging users to print posters designed by the group as stickers and distribute them locally, to which several people responded and posted videos of themselves carrying out these activities.

Conclusion

This chapter has examined how extreme-right online communities in Southeast Asia, particularly the Austronesian supremacist community, use memes as a tool to normalise extremist ideologies and narratives. While evidently influenced by the visual aesthetics and narratives of the Western extreme-right meme subculture, the community actively adapts these elements to reflect the local context, making them resonant and appealing to regional audiences. The chapter also unpacked the ideological heterogeneity of the community, revealing subgroups that go beyond the predominant ethno-nationalist monolith, blending elements of the extreme right with other extremist ideologies.

Furthermore, it shows how online communities facilitate the sharing and reinforcement of extremist beliefs by building a sense of community. Memes play a crucial role here, clearly demarcating the in-groups and out-groups and solidifying group cohesion. Additionally, community building occurs through the creation of online groups on encrypted platforms, where more explicit content can be shared. This could potentially facilitate recruitment and radicalisation, and in the longer term encourage real-world mobilisation.

The emergence of such extreme-right online communities, even those in the nascent stage, should concern policymakers for several reasons. Scholar J.M. Berger reminds us that "the root cause of terrorism is extremism".[26] In other words, extremism is almost exclusively the precursor to acts of terror. Furthermore, Berger points out that while not all extremists resort to violence, these movements can shift between violent and non-violent phases depending on the capabilities of the extremists and the environment they operate in.[27] Hence, while the extreme-right online community in SEA may not currently be in a violent phase, this does not preclude the possibility of future violence, as circumstances and material conditions can change.

Such a shift has already occurred in the West, with documented terrorist incidents involving white supremacist shooters demonstrably linked to the extreme-right meme subculture. For example, Christchurch shooter Brenton Tarrant was demonstrably immersed in this subculture, as evidenced by references to it in his manifesto and acts of violence. With the diffusion of this subculture into SEA, its role as a contributing factor towards violent extremism could feasibly expand beyond the West.

Furthermore, it should be noted that attraction to these extreme-right online communities does not occur in a vacuum. Joe Whittaker emphasised the problematic dichotomy between the "online" and "offline" spheres, given their interconnected nature.[28] In other words, understanding why these users become radicalised or are attracted to the community requires consideration of the broader "offline" environment, such as personal behaviours and motivations.[29]

Therefore, while policymakers continue efforts to moderate and ban these extreme-right accounts – a strategy that may be effective as a short-term solution – it is arguably a temporary fix that fails to address the core issue: why these users are drawn to such a community and environment in the first place. To achieve more sustainable change, policymakers should therefore not only expand existing PCVE tools to include counter-narratives specifically targeting the extreme right but also develop comprehensive social engagement strategies that consider "offline" social, economic, and psychological factors beyond the digital realm.

Endnotes

1. Taking cue from the works of Julia Ebner, the extreme right refers to individuals or groups that exhibit "at least three of the following five features: nationalism, racism, xenophobia, anti-democracy, and strong state advocacy". For more, see J. Ebner, *Going Dark: The Secret Social Lives of Extremists* (London: Bloomsbury Publishing, 2020).
2. "Indonesian students evict Rohingya from shelter demanding deportation", *Al Jazeera*, December 27, 2023. https://www.aljazeera.com/news/2023/12/27/indonesian-students-evict-rohingya-from-shelter-demanding-deportation.

3. In mid-March 2024, images of socks bearing the word "Allah" being sold at a KK Super Mart in Bandar Sunway, Selangor, went viral on social media. The incident led to a national outcry, with Malaysians, particularly Malay Muslims, questioning the insensitivity of selling such items. This sparked immediate backlash and boycott calls from online users who viewed the socks as sacrilegious. For more, see S. Shukri, "The risks and perceived rewards of rising revivalist populism in Malaysia", *Fulcrum*, May 16, 2024. https://fulcrum.sg/the-risks-and-perceived-rewards-of-rising-revivalist-populism-in-malaysia/.
4. K. Ramakrishna, "Understanding Singapore's 'multicultural white supremacists'", *RSIS*, January 29, 2024. https://www.rsis.edu.sg/rsis-publication/rsis/understanding-singapores-multicultural-white-supremacists/.
5. M. Mustaffa, "Radical right activities in Nusantara's digital landscape: A snapshot", Report-GNET (The Global Network on Extremism and Technology (GNET)), April 19, 2022. https://gnet-research.org/wp-content/uploads/2022/04/GNET-Report-Radical-Right-Activities-in-Nusantaras-Digital-Landscape.pdf.
6. J. S. Sarwono, "'Yup, another far-right classic': The propagation of far-right content on TikTok in Malaysia, Indonesia, and the Philippines", *GNET*, November 8, 2023. https://gnet-research.org/2023/11/08/yup-another-far-right-classic-the-propagation-of-far-right-content-on-tiktok-in-malaysia-indonesia-and-the-philippines/.
7. "Memes & the extreme right-wing", *Institute for Strategic Dialogue*, February 23, 2023. https://www.isdglobal.org/explainers/memes-the-extreme-right-wing/.
8. C. Thorleifsson, "From cyberfascism to terrorism: On 4chan/Pol/Culture and the transnational production of memetic violence", *Nations and Nationalism*, 28(1), 291 (2022). https://doi.org/10.1111/nana.12780.
9. U. K. Schmid, H. Schulze, and A. Drexel, "Memes, humor, and the far right's strategic mainstreaming", *Information, Communication & Society*, 1–3, April 10, 2024. https://doi.org/10.1080/1369118X.2024.2329610.
10. This observation is based on anecdotal examples from the author's research, which include social media content featuring the users themselves, references to masculinity, and occasional mentions of school.
11. S. Basha, "The creeping influence of the extreme right's meme subculture in Southeast Asia's TikTok community", *GNET*, April 8, 2024. https://gnet-research.org/2024/04/08/the-creeping-influence-of-the-extreme-rights-meme-subculture-in-southeast-asias-tiktok-community/.
12. *Ibid.*
13. Sarwono (2023). *Op. cit.*
14. Basha (2024). *Op. cit.*
15. The "Great Replacement" conspiracy theory posits that white Christian nations in the West are under threat of being overrun and undermined by non-White populations through immigration and higher birth rates.

16. Basha (2024). *Op. cit.*; J. S. Sarwono, "Tracing Austronesian supremacy rhetoric on social media: Its impact on the fate of Rohingya refugees", *GNET*, May 28, 2024. https://gnet-research.org/2024/05/28/tracing-austronesian-supremacy-rhetoric-on-social-media-its-impact-on-the-fate-of-rohingya-refugees/.
17. Sarwono (2024). *Op. cit.*
18. Basha (2024). *Op. cit.*
19. A. Meleagrou-Hitchens and M. Ayad, "The age of incoherence? Understanding mixed and unclear ideology extremism", Program on Extremism, George Washington University; and National Counterterrorism Innovation, Technology, and Education Center, Reports, Projects, and Research, June 7, 2023. https://digitalcommons.unomaha.edu/ncitereportsresearch/41.
20. Meleagrou-Hitchens and Ayad (2023). *Op. cit.*
21. Observations and data used in this segment were obtained from the author's personal research as a research analyst in ICPVTR.
22. A.-M. Bliuc *et al.*, "The growing power of online communities of the extreme-right: Deriving strength, meaning, and direction from significant socio", in *Real Life*, n.d., 3.
23. *Ibid.*, 3–4.
24. Thorleifsson (2022). *Op. cit.*, 290.
25. Observations and data used in this segment were obtained from the author's personal research as a research analyst in ICPVTR.
26. J. M. Berger, "Researching violent extremism: The state of play", *Resolve Network, Researching Violent Extremism Series*, 2, June 28, 2019. https://www.rcc.int/p-cve/download/docs/RSVE_RVESeries_ResearchingViolentExtremism-TheStateofPlay_JMBerger_June2019.pdf/2a2378fb048c5aeb57229352f3b71dbb.pdf.
27. *Ibid.*, 4.
28. J. Whittaker, "Rethinking online radicalization", 16(4), 74 (2022).
29. *Ibid.*, 78.

© 2025 Nanyang Technological University
https://doi.org/10.1142/9789819812691_0003

CHAPTER 3

Far-Right Extremism and Singaporean Youths – Countermeasures and Implications for Decision/Policymakers

Muhammad Haziq Bin Jani

Key Points
- Two cases of Singaporean youths self-radicalised by far-right extremism underscore the global nature of the far-right extremism (FRE) threat, the potency of its online presence, and its ability to inspire non-white involvement.
- Political ideologies or religious beliefs that encourage the upheaval of peaceful political processes in favour of majoritarian dominance, as well as hatred of minorities and vulnerable communities, need to be monitored closely.
- Hatred, racism, and imaginations of ethno-religious supremacy can "cross-pollinate" across different political and socio-cultural contexts and can be localised to fit specific perceptions of existential threat and myths of the past.

- Building understanding and trust between majority–minority and privileged–vulnerable communities can inoculate societies from susceptibility to extremist ideologies.
- Unless political discourse in the West arrives at a new equilibrium, it will continue to be a fount of FRE rhetoric and ideology.

Introduction

Since 9/11, global attention towards terrorism had understandably focussed on the threat posed by Salafi-jihadist groups such as Al-Qaeda (AQ) and the Islamic State (ISIS). However, over the past decade, far-right extremism (FRE) and political violence have emerged as a growing security concern, particularly in Europe and the US. Since 2020, the United Nations Counter-Terrorism Committee Executive Directorate (CTED) has increasingly identified incidents of political violence and terrorism related to FRE. Recently, in its 2024 Global Terrorism Threat Assessment, the Center for Strategic and International Studies (CSIS) highlighted that far-right extremism and violence were no longer a domestic terror concern in the West and that extremist groups and networks had driven political violence and the spread of far-right extremist ideologies internationally. Two cases of Singaporean youths self-radicalised by far-right extremism underscore the global nature of the FRE threat, the potency of its online presence, and its ability to inspire non-white involvement.

Focus on Countering Violent Extremism

It has been rightly pointed out that terminologies such as "right wing" and "far right" do little to describe the entire range of phenomena that are given the label, from xenophobic identitarians in Europe and white supremacists in the US to Christian extremists, as well as Hindu nationalists in India and Buddhist movements in Myanmar and Sri Lanka.[1] While definitions remain imprecise, ideologically, these groups exhibit a nativist nationalism, ethnonationalist xenophobia, and racism.[2] They may also be hostile to or explicitly reject democracy.[3] Hence, in addressing the FRE threat, policymakers in Singapore should be broadly vigilant against political ideologies or religious beliefs that encourage the upheaval of peaceful political processes in favour of majoritarian dominance, as well as hatred of minorities and vulnerable communities. As will be explained in the following, the nature of FRE appeal and its cross-pollination to non-West/white contexts necessitates a fair-handed but firm approach against all forms of extremism, paying attention to ideologies and particular narratives that are detrimental to what Singapore prizes – social cohesion and inter-group harmony – rather than dismissing the larger package of extremism as being manifestly foreign or irrelevant to our society.

Non-White Involvement is Not Improbable

Both Singaporean cases of FRE self-radicalisation point to the West as the present source and focal point of far-right extremist ideologies. However, the cases also demonstrate the infectious potential of FRE – in its Western, white, and "Christian" form – across ethnic differences and socio-cultural contexts. In the first case of FRE-inspired self-radicalisation, the individual of Indian ethnicity had watched the livestream of the 2019 Christchurch attack, developed a strong hatred towards Islam, and had prepared a message – which was intended to be disseminated prior to his planned attack – that was addressed to the people of France and in response to the 2020 Nice stabbings.[4]

In the second case, the 16-year-old of Chinese ethnicity who identified as a white supremacist had first chanced upon US far-right political commentator Paul Nicholas Miller and eventually developed hatred towards communities typically targeted by far-right extremists including African Americans and Arab immigrants.[5]

The radicalisation of non-white youths in Singapore mirrors the broader phenomenon of non-white involvement in far-right politics and violence in the US, which is referred to as "multicultural white supremacy". For instance, the 2023 Texas mass shooting and a separate attempted attack on the White House were conducted by non-white white supremacists Mauricio Garcia and Sai Varshith Kandula who are ethnically Hispanic and Indian, respectively.[6] Far-right political parties and extremist groups espouse more than just the idea of white supremacy. They also stoke fears that Christianity is under threat or that the "nation" has to "defend itself" from outsiders who are perpetrating crimes or damaging the political, economic, and moral order.[7] This multicultural form of fascism resonates with non-white Americans, and elements of this rhetoric – particularly anti-Muslim hatred and the Great Replacement narrative – can appeal to non-whites outside of the US context. It is also worth noting that the radicalisation process of an individual is complex, and other factors such as the relative youth of the Singaporean cases also played a role in their "falling prey".[8]

The Fluidity of Hatred and Supremacism

Hatred, racism, and imaginations of ethno-religious supremacy can "cross-pollinate" across different political and socio-cultural contexts and can be localised to fit specific perceptions of existential threat and myths of the past. In contexts where Muslims are perceived as a threat to the majority – such as in India or Myanmar – anti-Muslim narratives are used to incite hatred and violence.⁹ In Malaysia and Indonesia, sympathy towards Rohingya refugees transformed into anti-immigrant hatred when online mis/disinformation became conflated with antisemitism, resulting in death threats, protests, and harassment.[10] There have also been non-violent instances of adaptation of Western symbols of ethno-nationalist supremacism, such as Nazi and neo-Nazi aesthetics, due to the lack of historical awareness.[11] Analysts have also pointed to online meme communities that use FRE symbolism to imagine a pan-Austronesian racial superiority, reproducing FRE xenophobia, anti-immigrant sentiments, conspiracy theories, and calls to violence in a more relatable symbolic language.[12] As Western security agencies shift their security paradigm from countering terrorism externally to dealing with internal threats of political violence, policymakers in the Southeast Asian region should also consider how seemingly distant ethnic supremacism and in-group/out-group hatred can impact extremist discourse in their respective countries.

FRE Needs to Be Dealt with Online and Offline

From the Christchurch attack and the 2021 storming of the Capitol to calls for genocide against Muslims in India and against the Rohingya refugees in Malaysia and Indonesia, as well as the self-radicalisation of the two Singaporean youths, analysts have highlighted the role of social media platforms as centres of FRE recruitment and radicalisation, loudhailers for FRE ideology, and enablers of violence.[13] While social media companies such as Meta and X have since caved in to calls for better regulation of their users and content moderation, including deplatforming FRE ideologues and prominent figures, FRE groups have moved on to less regulated platforms such as Telegram, Reddit, Parler, and Gab in addition to FRE-friendly online forums such as 4chan, 8chan,

Discord, and Twitch where secluded forum spaces host content that is more extreme than what is found on mainstream social media.[14] FRE users of mainstream platforms such as TikTok are also savvy with the use of imagery and words that evade detection by artificial intelligence tools. This necessitates better policing of content by moderators that are attuned to the nuanced language and symbolism of our region.[15] Nevertheless, governments should continue to put pressure on social media companies to ensure that their platforms are safe spaces, even if these companies have to play catch-up with all sorts of extremists.

Beyond the regulation of online spaces, researchers also highlight the importance of building harmonious relations between communities in plural societies offline.[16] As pathways of radicalisation are facilitated by, inter alia, online and offline relationships, emotion and affect, and individual factors, building understanding and trust between majority–minority and privileged–vulnerable communities can inoculate societies from susceptibility to extremist ideologies.[17] FRE ideas about cultural differences and the socio-political order are antithetical to the spirit of multiculturalism in plural, multicultural, and multireligious societies. Whereas inclusivist societies such as Singapore have worked towards reducing inequalities based on ethnicity, immigration status, and gender and eliminating politicisation and polarisation based on difference, FRE is hostile towards such programs and is directed to maintaining or even augmenting inequalities in favour of the "natives".[18] FRE functions on the notion of ethnopluralism, which seeks to preserve the elusive national characters of people by keeping them separate, or by expelling those who are not of the same identity or who do not fit in.[19] This explains why immigrants and Muslims have been the target of FRE hatred and violence in the US, Europe, Australia, and New Zealand, and why notions of social cohesion are besieged by FRE, where expectations of "integration" are really a mask for separation, expulsion, and hate.[20] Hence, governments addressing the FRE threat should work towards notions of inclusivity, multiculturalism, and "transculturalism" that emphasise the mutability and dynamism of culture, eliminate the essentialism of identities and differences, and encourage social groups to encounter each other, learn from one another, and develop progressive and productive social relations.[21] To this end, Singapore's emphasis on social cohesion by engendering social encounters through public policies and encouraging inter-group understanding and dialogue is a model approach, which nevertheless needs to keep up with evolving domestic social dynamics.[22] Singapore's own two cases of youth FRE radicalisation are reminders that it is still possible for individuals to fall through the cracks.

Reflecting on the domestic-transnational nature of FRE and how FRE ideology can be "cross-pollinated" and glocalised, policymakers can also consider the role of international platforms and programmes, such as ASEAN Identity and the International Conference on Cohesive Societies (ICCS), in fostering regional understanding through cultural exchanges and cooperation. Perhaps, multicultural dialogue and encounters at that level may also help dampen the persuasiveness of extremist mis/disinformation and hate campaigns, as well as narratives of ethno-cultural or religious supremacy.

Conclusion

Far-right rhetoric is becoming firmly mainstream in the US and Europe with far-right political parties and organisations gaining traction or holding ground. Mis/disinformation and online anti-immigrant and Islamophobic campaigns following the July 2024 Southport stabbings triggered riots and violence across the United Kingdom, amplified by social media platform algorithms and comments by prominent bad actors and influencers such as Elon Musk.[23] Under the second Trump

Administration, the US has also witnessed further normalisation of far-right extremism. On his first day, US president Donald Trump pardoned more than 1,500 defendants charged over the 6 January 2021 "insurrection".[24] During Trump's post-swearing in inauguration rally, Musk made a straight-arm gesture reminiscent of a Nazi salute, which was reportedly celebrated by the extreme far-right.[25] These developments have only energized far-right extremists, who see the next four years as their period of "awakening".[26] Unless political discourse in the West arrives at a new equilibrium, it will continue to be a fount of FRE rhetoric and ideology. It will take more than a decade for political discourse in the West to push far-right and right-wing rhetoric out of the mainstream and even longer for FRE to be expunged from the "dark corners of the web" where it currently thrives.

Endnotes

1. L. Farrow, "Rise of the far-right: Too broad a category?", *RSIS Commentary*, April 11, 2022. https://www.rsis.edu.sg/rsis-publication/rsis/rise-of-the-far-right-too-broad-a-category/.
2. J. Rydgren, "The sociology of the radical right", *Annual Review of Sociology*, 33, 241–62 (2007).
3. C. Mudde, *The Ideology of the Extreme Right* (Manchester: Manchester University Press, 2000).
4. Internal Security Department, "Detention of Singaporean youth who intended to attack Muslims on the anniversary of Christchurch attacks in New Zealand", January 27, 2021. https://www.mha.gov.sg/mediaroom/press-releases/detention-of-singaporean-youth-who-intended-to-attack-muslims-on-the-anniversary-of-christchurch-attacks-in-new-zealand/.
5. Internal Security Department, "Update on terrorism-related cases under the internal security act", January 24, 2024. https://www.mha.gov.sg/mediaroom/press-releases/update-on-terrorism-related-cases-under-the-internal-security-act-24-january-2024/.
6. "Why 'white' supremacists are not always white", *Al Jazeera*, June 2, 2023. https://www.aljazeera.com/opinions/2023/6/2/why-white-supremacists-are-not-always-white.
7. V. Srivastava and D. M. HoSang, "Why are brown and black people supporting the far right", *The Conversation*, October 5, 2023. https://theconversation.com/why-are-brown-and-black-people-supporting-the-far-right-214800.

8. K. Ramakrishna, "Understanding Singapore's 'multicultural white supremacists'", *RSIS Commentary*, January 29, 2024. https://www.rsis.edu.sg/rsis-publication/rsis/understanding-singapores-multicultural-white-supremacists/.
9. E. Leidig, "Hindutva as a variant of right-wing extremism", *Patterns of Prejudice*, 54(3) (2020); A. Gunasingham, "Myanmar's extreme Buddhist nationalists", *The Interpreter*, September 21, 2021. https://www.lowyinstitute.org/the-interpreter/myanmar-s-extreme-buddhist-nationalists.
10. M. H. B. Jani, "Transnational hate speech and disinformation: Anti-Rohingya sentiments in Indonesia", *IDSS Paper*, January 24, 2024. https://www.rsis.edu.sg/rsis-publication/idss/ip24008-transnational-hate-speech-and-disinformation-anti-rohingya-sentiments-in-indonesia/.
11. M. Mustaffa, "Right-wing extremism has deep roots in Southeast Asia", *Global Network on Extremism and Technology (GNET) Insights*, July 14, 2021. https://gnet-research.org/2021/07/14/right-wing-extremism-has-deep-roots-in-southeast-asia/.
12. S. Basha, "The creeping influence of the extreme right's meme subculture in Southeast Asia's TikTok community", *Global Network on Extremism and Technology (GNET) Insights*, April 8, 2024. https://gnet-research.org/2024/04/08/the-creeping-influence-of-the-extreme-rights-meme-subculture-in-southeast-asias-tiktok-community/.
13. S. Leitch and P. Pickering, *Rethinking Social Media and Extremism* (Canberra: ANU Press, 2022); J. S. Sarwono, "Tracing Austronesian supremacy rhetoric on social media: Its impact on the fate of Rohingya refugees", *Global Network on Extremism and Technology (GNET) Insights*, May 28, 2024. https://gnet-research.org/2024/05/28/tracing-austronesian-supremacy-rhetoric-on-social-media-its-impact-on-the-fate-of-rohingya-refugees/; "India's Hindu extremists are calling for genocide against Muslims. Why is little being done to stop them?", *CNN*, January 14, 2022. https://edition.cnn.com/2022/01/14/asia/india-hindu-extremist-groups-intl-hnk-dst/index.html.
14. T. Munk, *Far-Right Extremism Online: Beyond the Fringe* (Abingdon, Oxon: Routledge, 2024); R. Scrivens, "Examining online behaviors of violent and non-violent right-wing extremists during peak posting days", *Studies in Conflict & Terrorism*, 1–24, May 5, 2024. https://www.tandfonline.com/doi/full/10.1080/1057610X.2024.2347860#abstract; O. Brown, "Right-wing extremism online: Can we use digital data to measure risk?", *Centre for Research and Evidence on Security Threats*, August 4, 2022. https://crestresearch.ac.uk/comment/right-wing-extremism-online-can-we-use-digital-data-to-measure-risk/.
15. Basha (2024). *Op. cit.*
16. P. Hedges, "Rise of violent Christian extremism: Whither inter-religious ties?", *RSIS Commentary*, February 11, 2021. https://www.rsis.edu.sg/rsis-publication/rsis/rise-of-violent-christian-extremism-whither-inter-religious-ties/; A. Marwick, B. Clancy, and K. Furl, "Far-right online radicalization: A review of the literature", *The Bulletin of Technology & Public Life* (2022). https://citap.pubpub.org/pub/jq7l6jny/release/1.

17. Marwick *et al*. (2022). *Op. cit.*; R. van Wonderen, D. Burggraaff, S. Ganpat, G. van Beek, and O. Cauberghs, "Right-wing extremist radicalisation on social media platforms?", August 2023. https://repository.wodc.nl/bitstream/handle/20.500.12832/3304/3341-rechtsextremisme-op-sociale-media-platforms-summary.pdf?sequence=3&isAllowed=y.
18. N. Bobbio, *Left and Right: The Significance of a Political Distinction* (Chicago: University of Chicago Press, 1996).
19. M. Fennema, "Populist parties of the right", in J. Rydgren (ed.) *Movements of Exclusion: Radical Right-Wing Populism in the Western World* (Hauppauge: Nova Science, 2005), pp. 1–24.
20. J. Lewis, P. Pond, R. Cameron, and B. Lewis, "Social cohesion, twitter and far-right politics in Australia: Diversity in the democratic mediasphere", *European Journal of Cultural Studies*, 22(5–6), 958–978 (2019).
21. J. Lewis, *Language Wars: The Role of Media and Culture in Global Terror and Political Violence* (London: Pluto Books, 2005); Lewis *et al*. (2019). *Op. cit.*
22. "More to social cohesion than just racial and religious harmony, says SMU President", *Straits Times*, September 6, 2022. https://www.straitstimes.com/singapore/more-to-social-cohesion-than-just-racial-and-religious-harmony-says-smu-president#:~:text=Home-,More%20to%20social%20cohesion%20than%20just,religious%20harmony%2C%20says%20SMU%20president&text=SINGAPORE%20%2D%20Social%20cohesion%20is%20not,building%20racial%20and%20religious%20harmony; "Building a cohesive society requires deliberate, consistent effort: DPM Lawrence Wong", *Straits Times*, September 8, 2022. https://www.straitstimes.com/singapore/politics/building-a-cohesive-society-requires-deliberate-consistent-effort-dpm-wong.
23. "Commentary: Why UK riots over southport child stabbings matter to Singapore", *CNA*, August 27, 2024. https://www.channelnewsasia.com/commentary/uk-riots-lessons-singapore-misinformation-disinformation-far-right-multi-cultural-racial-society-4570006#:~:text=It's%20been%20a%20number%20of,among%20other%20cities%2C%20are%20stern.
24 C. Gallagher, "Trump's pardons suggest he will run a far-right government with paramilitary backing", *London School of Economics – United States Politics and Policy*, February 7, 2025. https://blogs.lse.ac.uk/usappblog/2025/02/07/trumps-pardons-suggest-he-will-run-a-far-right-government-with-paramilitary-backing/.
25 B. Condon, "Musk's straight-arm gesture embraced by right-wing extremists regardless of what he meant", January 22, 2025. https://apnews.com/article/musk-gesture-salute-antisemitism-0070dae53c7a73397b104ae645877535.
26 B. Makuch, "Energized neo-Nazis feel their moment has come as Trump changes everything", *The Guardian*, January 26, 2025. https://www.theguardian.com/us-news/2025/jan/26/neo-nazis-trump-extremism.

PART 2

HINDUTVA

© 2025 Nanyang Technological University
https://doi.org/10.1142/9789819812691_0004

CHAPTER 4

Hindutva's Global Appeal – Recent Developments

Antara Chakraborthy

Key Points
- Hindutva's rise has been accompanied by concerns regarding its association with right-wing extremism.
- A major factor contributing to Hindutva's local appeal is the BJP's effective politicisation of religious identities and perceived historical grievances in Indian history.
- Hindutva's role in cultural preservation and identity formation among the Indian diasporic community (especially youth) contributes to its global appeal.
- The portrayal of Hindutva as a counterforce to perceived threats from other minority religious factions can also resonate with the broader nationalist conservative movements.
- While Hindutva does enjoy support among sections of the Indian diaspora, it also faces opposition.

Introduction

India's prime minister, Narendra Modi, ushered the ruling Bharatiya Janata Party in a victory for the third term in June 2024.[1] This is a significant feat in India for two reasons: (1) Narendra Modi is only the second Prime Minister in India, after Jawaharlal Nehru, to win three consecutive terms[2] and (2) this year's electoral victory further cements BJP's dominance in India's electoral landscape.

India, often called the "World's largest democracy",[3] has been under a lot of scrutiny in the last decade for its growing rise in Hindu nationalism.[4] Since 2014, when BJP first secured its first big victory under Modi's leadership, Hindu nationalism – built upon the ideology of *Hindutva* – has surged into the mainstream.[5] *Hindutva*, a political ideology, has its roots in the 19th century, taking shape amidst the then-evolving diverse fabric of British India.[6] At its core, it asserts that the "Indian national identity" and culture are intricately tied to the religion of Hinduism.[7] The ideology further gained significant traction in the early 20th century, coinciding with India's independence movement, which aimed to assert independence from British colonial rule.

The word Hindutva, loosely translated to *"Hindu-ness"*, was coined in the 1920s by Vinayak Damodar Savarkar and has emerged as the dominant form of Hindu nationalism in India.[8] In his pamphlet "Essentials of Hindutva",[9] Savarkar called for Hindus to come together as one homogenous community and "reclaim" their ancient homeland from those he considered "outsiders", which included people from other religions in India, especially Muslims.[10] Hinduism, as a religion, is vastly diverse and varies from region to region, keeping in mind the cultural makeup of India. This exercise, apart from being exclusionary to "outsiders", homogenises the Hindu community.[11] Another central tenet of Hindutva is the staunch belief in the pre-eminence of Hinduism in Indian society and the desire to establish the nation (*Rashtra*) as explicitly Hindu rather than secular.[12] MS Golwalkar, another Hindutva ideologue, expanded this ideology to define Hindus as a "race" of people tied together by a common geography, culture, and religion.[13] Within this framework, Hindus are regarded more as an ethnic community than merely followers of a religion.

However, Hindutva's rise has been accompanied by concerns regarding its association with right-wing extremism.[14] To a large degree, the popularity of Modi can be attributed to the effective way in which the BJP has capitalised on these Hindutva narratives and politicised religious identities in India. Critics point to Hindutva's purist racial undertones and its propensity for intolerance towards religious and ethnic minorities, particularly Muslims.[15] This intolerance has manifested in instances of anti-Muslim sentiment and violence, particularly in a nation where Hindus form the majority, constituting around 80% of the population, while Muslims make up approximately 14%.[16]

One example of this is the BJP's emphasis on issues like the construction of the Ram Temple in Ayodhya. This project, which reached its final stages in January 2024,[17] has been a long-standing demand of Hindu nationalist groups and serves as a powerful symbol of Hindu resurgence.[18] The temple, built upon the demolished Babri Masjid wrecked by Hindutva mobs in 1992, led to widespread communal violence across the country, highlighting the volatile intersection of religion and politics – especially between the Hindu and Muslim communities.[19] The BJP's continued commitment to building the temple has been instrumental in rallying support from proponents of Hindutva.

Another example of the BJP leveraging Hindutva ideology for political gain is the Citizenship Amendment Act (CAA)[20] passed in 2019. The CAA provides a pathway to Indian citizenship for non-Muslim refugees from Pakistan, Bangladesh, and Afghanistan, which critics argue discriminates against Muslims and undermines India's secular constitution.[21] This legislation sparked nationwide protests and was seen as a move to further marginalise the Muslim community.[22]

Therefore, by politicising religious identities, Modi and the BJP have effectively tapped into a sense of cultural pride and victimhood among many Hindus. This approach not only secures their electoral base but also reshapes the national discourse, making Hindutva a dominant force in contemporary Indian politics.

Hindutva's Domestic Appeal

One of the most important aspects contributing to the popularity and success of Hindutva as a mainstream political movement in India lies in the BJP's effective politicisation of religious identities and perceived historical grievances in Indian history. Therefore, the rise of Hindutva cannot be discussed without examining the simultaneous rise of the BJP. The BJP's enormous growth and success as a political party in India can similarly be attributed to making the Hindu nationalist ideology resonate with the masses, normalising the rise of the far right within India's political landscape.[23]

Several important factors contribute to the broad appeal of Hindutva. Firstly, as mentioned previously, it taps into a deep-seated sense of cultural and religious identity among many Hindus, in India and in diasporic communities abroad, fostering pride in Hindu traditions and history. But this sense of pride is usually coupled with an emphasis on Hinduism as the cornerstone of Indian civilisation.[24] Secondly, political mobilisation has been pivotal in mainstreaming Hindutva, as BJP positioned itself as the protector of Hindu interests against perceived threats from religious minorities, particularly Muslims.[25] This narrative is further reinforced through grassroots campaigns, social media, and mass rallies. Herein, a lot of BJP's success in framing the narrative is also due to its expertise in combining governance with Hindutva through which it has introduced economic reforms and welfare schemes that appeal to a broad group of the populace.[26] Initiatives such as the Pradhan Mantri Awas Yojana (Housing for All)[27] and the success of Modi's flagship Swachh Bharat Abhiyan (Clean India Mission)[28] are some examples of these schemes that have helped broaden the party's appeal beyond its core base. And lastly, Modi's charismatic leadership also significantly contributes to the appeal of Hindutva, with his image as a strong, decisive leader who can restore India's past glory resonating with many, both within India's borders and outside.[29]

Hindutva's Global Appeal and Youth

The Indian diasporic community, particularly in countries like the US, Canada, the UK, and Australia, has shown enormous support for Modi and the BJP, often resonating with themes of Hindu pride and nationalism, which is contextualised within the community's lived experiences as a racial minority in host countries. This community has also become increasingly influential in political and economic spheres. For instance, several BJP-affiliated organisations in the US like the Hindu American Foundation (HAF) and the Overseas Friends of BJP (OFBJP), to name a few, have actively promoted Hindutva-aligned policies and narratives. These groups engage in lobbying efforts, campaign contributions, and grassroots mobilisation to influence local and national politics in their host countries.[30]

Relatedly, the ideology of Hindutva shares certain characteristics with right-wing and nationalist movements, such as a clear emphasis on cultural identity, nationalism, and opposition to multiculturalism, couched under the rising tide of Islamophobia.[31] This has led to some degree of alignment and mutual support between Hindu nationalist supporters and other nationalist groups worldwide, where they often collaborate on issues such as immigration policy, religious freedom, and counterterrorism, which resonate with both Hindu nationalists and other right-wing groups.[32] In the UK for example, the National Council of Hindu Temples (NCHT), an umbrella body of over 100 temples, came under scrutiny in 2016 for hosting an event that invited Tommy Robinson, the leader of the English Defence League (EDL), a far-right group, as one of its speakers.[33]

Another reason for Hindutva's global appeal is its role in cultural preservation and identity formation among the Indian diasporic community.[34] For many immigrants, maintaining a connection to their cultural and religious roots is essential, and Hindutva provides a framework for this connection, emphasising Hindu traditions, festivals, and values.[35] Hindutva is thus intertwined with the broader desire of diasporic communities to sustain their heritage in their host countries.

The BJP's active outreach with the diasporic communities abroad and its ability to instil a sense of pride and belonging among Hindus have been instrumental in the mainstreaming of Hindutva within those communities.[36] The appeal of Hindutva, particularly in the context of BJP's brand, has played a crucial role in cultural preservation and identity formation among some of the younger generation of the Hindu Indian diaspora.[37] Many second- and third-generation immigrants seek to maintain a connection to their cultural and religious roots, and the rhetoric of Hindutva provides a framework for this connection. Cultural programmes, festivals, and community events centred on Hindu traditions serve as vital opportunities for the youth to engage with their heritage, fostering a sense of belonging and pride. Here, the BJP's outreach efforts have been instrumental in cultivating this connection and reinforcing this sense of cultural nationalism.[38]

The appeal of Hindu nationalism among the youth is also influenced by the socio-political dynamics in their host countries. In multicultural societies, many youth from Indian-origin diasporic communities have faced the complexities of identity politics.[39] Hindutva provides a unifying cultural identity that distinguishes them from other racial groups, offering a sense of solidarity against discrimination and marginalisation, positioning their cultural identity as a source of pride and strength.[40] This emphasis on community resonates particularly well as the youth often feel a sense of disconnect in their multicultural environments. However, when the political undercurrents of this movement are overlooked, it translates into openly celebrating Hindu nationalist ideals, as seen during events like the inauguration of the Ram Temple when saffron flags were waved in Times Square,[41] symbols that carry divisive meanings and reflect the growing polarisation in India, particularly against Muslim communities.[42]

The global appeal of Hindutva is also facilitated by sophisticated communication strategies and the effective use of media, where social media platforms, in particular, have become crucial tools for the dissemination of Hindutva ideologies.[43] As mentioned above, some members of diasporic communities in multicultural societies, navigating complex identity politics, see Hindutva as a unifying identity within these spaces.[44] This distinction becomes particularly relevant within the context of rising Islamophobia in the West, where Hindutva's emphasis on the Hindu identity can offer a sense of security and solidarity to Hindus. The portrayal of Hindutva as a counterforce to perceived threats from other minority religious factions can also resonate with the broader nationalist conservative movements.

Conclusion

As India emerges as a significant global player, its growing economic power and soft-power initiatives have gained more attention and influence.[45] Modi, especially in the last decade, has ramped up his engagement with the diaspora by promoting yoga, Ayurveda, etc., on the global stage, which can be linked to Hindu cultural practices, further enhancing India's soft power.[46] This cultural diplomacy, supported by the Indian government, has reinforced the appeal of Hindutva by presenting it as part of India's rich cultural heritage.[47]

However, Hindutva's association with religious intolerance and incidents of violence against minorities, particularly Muslims, within India have drawn criticism from various international human rights organisations and some foreign governments.[48] Reports of mob lynchings,[49] discrimination, and communal riots[50] have circulated in the news regularly and have raised alarm globally. The rise of Hindutva and its potential impact on regional stability, particularly in South Asia, are also being closely monitored.[51] Policies and actions perceived as exclusionary or aggressive towards minorities can affect India's diplomatic relations and its image on the world stage.[52] It must also be noted here that while Hindutva does enjoy support among sections of the Indian diaspora, it also faces opposition. Many in the diaspora advocate for a secular and inclusive India and oppose the BJP's policies and rhetoric.

Hindutva's rise, facilitated by the BJP and Modi, has led to significant shifts, reflecting broader discourses on nationalism, religious identity, and democratic values.[53] Its role as a political movement and ideology has played a pivotal role in shaping the contemporary Indian political landscape. Hindu nationalism has not only seen support within the domestic populace of India but has also resonated with many members of Indian diasporic communities worldwide, creating a sense of identity and solidarity among overseas Indians. This global reach has contributed to a transnational exchange on nationalism, intertwining with other right-wing movements across the globe.

Endnotes

1. K. Pathi and S. Saaliq, "Modi wins 3rd term in India's general election, narrowly securing majority", *PBS News,* June 4, 2024. https://www.pbs.org/newshour/world/modi-wins-3rd-term-in-indias-general-election-narrowly-securing-majority.
2. A. Sharma, "The first third term PM since Jawaharlal Nehru – why does Narendra Modi keep winning?", *Indian Express*, June 6, 2024. https://indianexpress.com/article/opinion/columns/narendra-modi-jawaharlal-nehru-winning-third-term-9375702/.
3. SOAS, "The Indian election: Is it still the world's largest democracy?" April 19, 2024. https://www.soas.ac.uk/about/blog/indian-election-it-still-worlds-largest-democracy.
4. M. Vaishnav, "The BJP in power: Indian democracy and religious nationalism", *Carnegie Endowment for International Peace*, April 4, 2019. https://carnegieendowment.org/research/2019/04/the-bjp-in-power-indian-democracy-and-religious-nationalism?lang=en.
5. K. Pathi and S. Saaliq, "India election: Hindu nationalism mainstream after Modi's decade in power", *AP News*, April 19, 2024. https://apnews.com/article/india-election-narendra-modi-hindu-nationalism-rss-79c30c8ae750a9c037d86b9e2c1b640c.
6. M. Basu, *The Rhetoric of Hindutva* (New York: Cambridge University Press, 2017). http://books.google.ie/books?id=E7gtDQAAQBAJ&printsec=frontcover&dq=The+Rhetoric+of+Hindutva&hl=&cd=1&source=gbs_api.
7. Ibid.
8. V. D. Savarkar, *Essentials of Hindutva* (India: Hindi Sahitya Sadan, 1922). https://library.bjp.org/jspui/bitstream/123456789/284/1/Essentials%20of%20Hindutva.pdf.
9. Ibid.
10. Ibid.

11. A. Truschke, "Hindutva appropriations of indigeneity", *SSRC the Immanent Frame*, October 17, 2022. https://tif.ssrc.org/2022/10/19/hindutva-appropriations-of-indigeneity/.
12. M. S. Golwalkar, *Bunch of Thoughts* (Sahitya Sindhu Prakashana, India: Rashtrotthana Sahitya, 1966). http://books.google.ie/books?id=c9_8EAAAQBAJ&printsec=frontcover&dq=MS+Golwalkar&hl=&cd=2&source=gbs_api.
13. *Ibid.*
14. E. Leidig, "Hindutva as a variant of right-wing extremism", *Patterns of Prejudice*, 54(3), 215–237 (2020). https://doi.org/10.1080/0031322X.2020.1759861.
15. A. Skaria, "Why Hindutva is a racist supremacism – not merely communalism or majoritarianism", *The Wire*, September 10, 2022. https://thewire.in/politics/why-hindutva-is-a-racist-supremacism-not-a-communalism-or-majoritarianism.
16. S. Biswas. "'Invisible in our own country': Being Muslim in Modi's India", April 28, 2024. https://www.bbc.com/news/world-asia-india-68498675; K. Schaeffer, "Key findings about the religious composition of India", *Pew Research Center*, April 14, 2024. https://www.pewresearch.org/short-reads/2021/09/21/key-findings-about-the-religious-composition-of-india/#:~:text=Hindus%20make%20up%2079.8%25%20of,declined%20by%20about%204%20points.
17. R. Mogul, V. Sud, S. Farooqui, A. S. Iyer, and J. Taylor, "India's Ayodhya Ram Mandir temple inaugurated by Modi", *CNN World*, January 22, 2024. https://edition.cnn.com/asia/live-news/india-ram-mandir-ayodhya-inauguration-24-01-22-intl-hnk/index.html.
18. A. S. Bardi, "Modi's India: How the New Ram Mandir Temple has transformed Ayodhya", *Foreign Policy*, March 5, 2024. https://foreignpolicy.com/2024/03/05/india-ram-mandir-ayodhya-modi-bjp-hindutva-elections/.
19. S. Saaliq, "India: A Hindu temple built atop a razed mosque is helping Modi's political standing", *AP News*, January 21, 2024. https://apnews.com/article/india-election-temple-modi-mosque-bjp-15d678e47f869a64993b724f905653b4.
20. Staff Reporter, "CAA: India's new citizenship law explained", *BBC*. March 12, 2024. https://www.bbc.com/news/world-asia-india-50670393.
21. *Ibid.*
22. S. Bhadoria, "What is CAA, the law which led to massive protests in 2019?" *Mint*, March 11, 2024. https://www.livemint.com/news/india/what-is-caa-the-law-which-led-to-massive-protests-in-2019-citizenship-amendment-act-all-you-need-to-know-11710172923021.html.
23. M. Vaishnav, "What is the secret to the success of India's Bharatiya Janata Party (BJP)?", *Carnegie Endowment for International Peace*, October 11, 2018. https://carnegieendowment.org/posts/2018/10/what-is-the-secret-to-the-success-of-indias-bharatiya-janata-party-bjp?lang=en.
24. A. Mitra, "Hindu civilization and Indian nationalism: Conceptual conflicts and convergences in the works of Romesh Chunder Dutt, c. 1870–1910", *Religions*, 14(8), 983 (2023). https://doi.org/10.3390/rel14080983.
25. S. Ammassari, "'We have thousands of Modis': The secret behind the BJP's enduring success in India", *The Conversation*, April 18, 2024. https://theconversation.com/

we-have-thousands-of-modis-the-secret-behind-the-bjps-enduring-success-in-india-227373.
26. S. Babar, "Hindu and Hindutva ideology in Indian Polity: Examining Modi's administration", *Strategic Studies*, 43(2), 80–96 (2024). https://doi.org/10.53532/ss.043.02.00301.
27. R. Chitlangia, "Modi 3.0 approves 3 cr more houses under PM Awas Yojana in rural & urban India", *The Print*, June 10, 2024. https://theprint.in/india/governance/modi-3-0-approves-3-cr-more-houses-under-pm-awas-yojana-in-rural-urban-india/2125499/.
28. D. Santdasani, "The Swachhta journey: New targets, new approaches", *Indian Express*, August 27, 2021. https://indianexpress.com/article/opinion/columns/swachh-bharat-mission-india-sanitation-amrut-7474128/.
29. S. Pal, "The making of the man's man: Stardom and the cultural politics of neoliberalism in Hindutva India", Order No. 28413108, Southern Illinois University at Carbondale, 2021. https://remotexs.ntu.edu.sg/user/login?url=https://www.proquest.com/dissertations-theses/making-man-s-stardom-cultural-politics/docview/2553540187/se-2.
30. R. De Souza, "Hindutva and ethnonationalism in the Indian American Diaspora", *Oxford Research Encyclopedia of Communication*, September 15, 2022. https://doi.org/10.1093/acrefore/9780190228613.013.1254.
31. E. Leidig, "Hindutva as a variant of right-wing extremism", *Patterns of Prejudice*, 54(3), 215–237 (2020). https://doi.org/10.1080/0031322X.2020.1759861.
32. S. Gandhi, "Hindutva and the shared scripts of the global right", *SSRC the Immanent Frame*, December 14, 2023. https://tif.ssrc.org/2022/10/12/hindutva-and-the-shared-scripts-of-the-global-right/; M. Daly, "How far-right Hindu supremacy went global", October 26, 2022. https://www.vice.com/en/article/n7z947/how-far-right-hindu-supremacy-went-global.
33. K. Hussein, "A Hindu temple has put a stop to an event featuring a former EDL leader", *BuzzFeed*, January 29, 2016. https://www.buzzfeed.com/husseinkesvani/a-hindu-temple-has-cancelled-an-event-that-featured; S. Bidwell, "Britain's Hindu nationalism problem", *The Critic Magazine*, August 15, 2023. https://thecritic.co.uk/britains-hindu-nationalism-problem/.
34. R. De Souza, "Hindutva and ethnonationalism in the Indian American Diaspora", *Oxford Research Encyclopaedia of Communication*, September 15, 2022. https://doi.org/10.1093/acrefore/9780190228613.013.1254.
35. Ibid.
36. R. de Souza and S. A. Hussain, "'Howdy Modi!': Mediatization, Hindutva, and long distance ethnonationalism", *Journal of International and Intercultural Communication*, 16(2), 138–61 (2021). https://doi.org/10.1080/17513057.2021.1987505.
37. A. Chakraborthy, "Hindu nationalism: Impact on multicultural societies", *RSIS Commentary*, March 7, 2023. https://www.rsis.edu.sg/rsis-publication/cens/hindu-nationalism-impact-on-multicultural-societies/.

38. D. Kapoor, "How Modi govt's outreach to Indian diaspora created a sense pride among them", *Organiser*, May 9, 2024. https://organiser.org/2024/05/09/236647/bharat/how-modi-govts-outreach-to-indian-diaspora-created-a-sense-pride-among-them/.
39. E. Anderson and A. Longkumer, "'Neo-Hindutva': Evolving forms, spaces, and expressions of Hindu nationalism", *Contemporary South Asia*, 26(4), 371–77 (2018). https://doi.org/10.1080/09584935.2018.1548576.
40. *Ibid.*
41. S. Sen, "Ayodhya celebrations at Times Square: Indian diaspora celebrates Ram Mandir ceremony", *Hindustan Times*, January 22, 2024. https://www.hindustantimes.com/world-news/us-news/ayodhya-celebrations-at-times-square-indian-diaspora-celebrates-ram-mandir-ceremony-101705894822806.html.
42. A. Banerji, "The Ram Mandir symbolizes a new form of Hinduism", *The Diplomat*, January 24, 2024. https://thediplomat.com/2024/01/the-ram-mandir-symbolizes-a-new-form-of-hinduism/.
43. *Ibid.*
44. R. Sengupta and P. Swamy, *Hindutva in Europe* (The Netherlands: BRILL eBooks, 2020), pp. 648–664. https://doi.org/10.1163/9789004432284_022.
45. D. Jaishankar, "India rising: Soft power and the world's largest democracy", *Brookings*, September 17, 2018. https://www.brookings.edu/articles/india-rising-soft-power-and-the-worlds-largest-democracy/.
46. *Ibid.*
47. R. Manuvie and A. Kahle, "Hindu nationalism on display in India's G20 presidency", *The Diplomat*, February 3, 2023. https://thediplomat.com/2023/02/hindu-nationalism-on-display-in-indias-g20-presidency/.
48. United States Department of State, "2023 Report on International Religious Freedom: India", June 26, 2024. https://www.state.gov/reports/2023-report-on-international-religious-freedom/india/.
49. S. Baksi and A. Nagarajan, "Mob lynchings in India: A look at data and the story behind the numbers", *Newslaundry*, July 4, 2017. https://www.newslaundry.com/2017/07/04/mob-lynchings-in-india-a-look-at-data-and-the-story-behind-the-numbers.
50. H. Ellis-Patterson, "Inside Delhi: Beaten, lynched and burnt alive", *The Guardian*, March 4, 2020. https://www.theguardian.com/world/2020/mar/01/india-delhi-after-hindu-mob-riot-religious-hatred-nationalists.
51. A. Malji, "The rise of Hindu nationalism and its regional and global ramifications", *Association for Asian Studies*, 23(1) (Spring 2018): Asian Politics. https://www.asianstudies.org/publications/eaa/archives/the-rise-of-hindu-nationalism-and-its-regional-and-global-ramifications/.
52. *Ibid.*
53. Vaishnav (2019). *Op. cit.*

© 2025 Nanyang Technological University
https://doi.org/10.1142/9789819812691_0005

CHAPTER 5

Hindutva and Social Cohesion in Singapore

Antara Chakraborthy

Key Points
- Indian diasporic communities in Southeast Asia are not immune to the growing appeal of Hindutva.
- The proliferation of political Hindu nationalist ideology is not a recent phenomenon but has seen a massive uptick in the last decade, with the rise of the Bharatiya Janata Party (BJP).
- The advent of social media and digital platforms has significantly amplified the reach of Hindutva ideologies.
- Continued vigilance is necessary as the inherent exclusionary nature of Hindutva poses significant and ongoing challenges to social cohesion and multiculturalism.
- Civil society organisations play a crucial role in helping inoculate society against divisive narratives and raising public awareness about the potential impact of Hindutva.

Introduction

The ideological underpinnings of Hindutva have resonated with the Indian diaspora worldwide, despite being primarily rooted within the Indian subcontinent.[1] In recent years, several Indian diasporic communities across the world, including the Southeast Asian region, have witnessed an increasing influence of Hindutva among their members.[2] This region, characterised by its history of multiracial coexistence and cultural diversity, presents a unique backdrop against which the rise of Hindutva can be studied.

Countries like Singapore[3] and Malaysia, within the broader Southeast Asian region, host a significant Indian population with deep-rooted cultural and religious ties to India, which have continued to evolve over time. The migration of Indians in this region dates back to colonial times, when the British brought in scores of Indians as indentured labourers. Subsequent waves of migration continued to enrich the local Indian community, forming an integral part of the social fabric of these nations.[4] However, these communities are not immune to the growing appeal of Hindutva. Although the proliferation of political Hindu nationalist ideology is not a recent phenomenon, it has seen a massive uptick in the last decade, especially with the rise of the Bharatiya Janata Party (BJP) in India.[5] This has further been bolstered by modern communication, social media, and transnational networks.

This chapter examines the appeal of Hindu nationalism in Singapore, its spread, and the subsequent responses from local governments and civil societies . These factors will help contribute to a deeper understanding of how global nationalist movements can influence and reshape local communities and whether they have the potential to alter the socio-cultural landscape of diverse regions like Southeast Asia.

The Potential Appeal of Hindutva in Singapore

In the last decade, particularly with the rise of BJP in India, Hindutva has seen a noticeable rise in its appeal and visibility among Indian diasporic communities across the world, including Singapore.[6] This phenomenon is multifaceted, driven by a complex interplay of political, cultural, and social factors that resonate with the local Indian community in host countries. One of the factors for this is the notion of cultural identity and preservation.

For many Hindus in Singapore, Hindu nationalism and the tenets of Hindutva offer a means to preserve and assert their cultural identity.[7] Having maintained strong ties to its heritage and the "motherland", the diaspora finds in Hindutva a framework that celebrates Hindu traditions and festivals . This cultural reaffirmation is significant in a multicultural society like Singapore, where the Indian community represents a minority. Hindutva's emphasis on "Hindu"[8] culture helps individuals feel a sense of belonging and pride in their heritage, further fostering a collective identity.[9]

However, in the Singapore context, it is essential to distinguish between Hindus from North and South India. There is a perspective that newer Indian migrants from North India may be more inclined to support Hindutva due to their familiarity with its narratives, language, and customs.[10] In contrast, individuals from South Indian communities might not traditionally align with Hindutva ideologies, often perceiving their cultural identity through other lenses, influenced by linguistic, regional, and caste-based differences. However, this does not imply that South Indian Hindus are immune to the influences of Hindutva.[11] Those who have lived in Singapore for generations may also find value in this rhetoric as it offers a meaningful connection to their heritage and culture.[12] This divergence highlights the complex dynamics within the Hindu community in Singapore, where varying perspectives on cultural identity coexist.

This further plays into the cultural shifts brought in by the rapid pace of globalisation. As traditional values and practices come under strain from global influences,[13] Hindutva provides a counter-narrative that emphasises traditional Hindu values and lifestyles.[14] This appeal to tradition is particularly effective for older generations who fear the erosion of their cultural norms. Similarly, for younger generations, Hindutva offers a way to reconnect with their roots, further reinforcing a sense of community and solidarity.[15] The promotion of a unified Hindu identity that transcends the diverse regional and linguistic differences among Indians remains a particularly appealing factor in multicultural settings.

Like most Indian diasporic communities across the world, the community in Singapore comprises people from various parts of India and Hindutva's emphasis on a common cultural and religious identity helps to bridge these internal divides.[16] This solidarity is continuously reinforced through community activities, religious gatherings, and cultural events that bring people together under the banner of Hindu nationalism. For instance, the inauguration of the controversial Ram Temple in Ayodhya in 2024 brought Hindu diasporic communities together globally. Festivities were organised from the United States to France and Australia, spearheaded by the Vishwa Hindu Parishad (VHP) – an affiliate of the RSS-BJP organisations – and other Hindu diaspora groups.[17] In Southeast Asia, VHP Thailand announced on X (previously Twitter) that Nagesh Singh, Ambassador and Permanent Representative to the UNESCAP, will attend the event at Dev Mandir Bangkok.[18] Similar celebrations were also planned in Singapore, Kuala Lumpur, Jakarta, and Bali.[19]

Here, it is important to note that Hindutva, first and foremost, is a political movement and not an extension of the Hindu religion, even though it is constantly conflated. Many among the Indian diaspora in Singapore, while integrated into the local socio-political fabric, remain connected to political developments in India.[20] The BJP and its affiliate organisations have effectively leveraged these connections, including high-profile visits by PM Narendra Modi, cultural programs, and diaspora-specific outreach events. These activities help to create a sense of political participation and influence among the diasporas. In fact, Modi's widespread popularity in the region earned him the title of "Asian of the Year 2014" by *The Straits Times*.[21]

Finally, the advent of social media and digital platforms has significantly amplified the reach of Hindutva ideologies.[22] Platforms like WhatsApp, Facebook, and YouTube serve as channels for disseminating nationalist and political content, and the Indian diaspora in Singapore, like its global counterparts, is highly active on these platforms.[23] For example, Hindu On Campus – an active social media page on X (formerly known as Twitter) – describes itself as "a space for diaspora Hindus fighting Hinduphobia". Managed by students, the page boasts 43k followers and focuses on Hindu-centric content. However, some of this content has been criticised for employing polarising and discriminatory language, particularly in how it frames discussions on Hinduism and Hindutva. Such language can create divisions within diasporic communities by presenting critiques of Hindutva as equivalent to attacks on Hinduism, reflecting broader tensions in the dialogue surrounding Hindu identity and nationalism.[24] The digital space allows for the rapid spread of Hindutva narratives, creating virtual communities that reinforce these ideologies. Social media influencers and digital activists[25] play a crucial role in shaping opinions and mobilising support for Hindutva within the diaspora.[26]

Government and Civil Society Organisations

Unlike in countries such as the US, UK, or Canada, where Hindutva has, at times, disrupted social harmony[27], Singapore has not yet experienced similar issues. As Singapore places utmost emphasis on its multiracial and multireligious makeup, the government has taken a vigilant approach to monitor and regulate any activities that can cause social division and polarisation.[28] The government has implemented several policies that are aimed at promoting cultural diversity and inclusivity. For example, initiatives such as the Racial and Religious Harmony Circles (RRHCs)[29] and the International Conference on Cohesive Societies (ICCS)[30] work at the grassroots level and facilitate conversations with religious leaders and scholars to monitor and mediate any inter-religious tensions. Interfaith dialogues such as these are crucial in fostering respect among different religious communities and countering exclusivist narratives promoted by movements like Hindutva.

Civil society organisations also play a pivotal role in promoting secular values and countering extremist ideologies. In Singapore, organisations like OnePeople.Sg work towards promoting racial harmony through various programs.[31]

However, continued vigilance is necessary as the inherent exclusionary nature of Hindutva poses significant and ongoing challenges to social cohesion and multiculturalism. While these aforementioned government initiatives have been effective in promoting social cohesion and diversity, they face the challenge of monitoring and regulating diaspora organisations with the potential perception of infringing upon religious freedoms.[32] The Indian diaspora in Singapore, though diverse, remains a significant part of the nation's social fabric, and the promotion of Hindutva's exclusionary ideas could potentially lead to tensions with other ethnic and religious groups, for instance, Hindu nationalism manifesting as islamophobia and threatening Singapore's social harmony.[33]

To maintain social cohesion and uphold diversity and inclusivity, it is crucial for relevant bodies to continue monitoring the spread of diasporic Hindu nationalism, as they would other forms of extremist thinking.[34] Continued support for initiatives promoting diversity and inclusivity will further strengthen Singapore's social fabric. By adopting a vigilant and proactive approach, Singapore can continue to cultivate a safe and equitable society that respects the fundamental rights and dignity of all individuals, regardless of their beliefs and origins.

Fostering Social Cohesion

Given the potential for Hindutva-related rhetoric to incite hatred and violence, as seen in the rising cases of targeted attacks on minorities in India, it is essential for Singapore to closely monitor and regulate hate speech, both online and offline. Singapore's existing legal framework, which includes the Maintenance of Religious Harmony Act, provides a foundation for addressing hate speech and promoting religious harmony.[35] Strengthening these measures and ensuring their consistent application can prevent the spread of harmful ideologies. It is also important to encourage social media platforms to take a proactive stance against hate speech to curtail the online dissemination of divisive rhetoric. Policymakers in Singapore must also be cognisant of the transnational nature of Hindutva[36] and other similar ideologies and strengthen digital literacy efforts.[37]

This must be enforced in tandem with a continuous effort to build social resilience. Building social resilience involves strengthening the capacity of the community to withstand and recover from divisive forces, and this is usually achieved through various community-building activities.[38] This encourages communities to feel a sense of ownership and responsibility and actively participate in shaping their social environments. This is crucial as it fosters a culture of inclusivity and mutual support, making society more resilient to the impact of divisive ideologies like Hindutva.[39] Singapore's Indian community, in particular, is diverse, with members hailing from various religious, linguistic, and cultural backgrounds.[40] Therefore, policymakers should engage with these communities, ensuring all voices are heard, encouraging cross-cultural interaction and collaboration among different Indian subgroups. Additionally, supporting the efforts of civil society organisations that promote inclusivity and social cohesion can complement government efforts. Civil society organisations play a crucial role in helping inoculate society against divisive narratives and raise public awareness about the potential impact of Hindutva.[41] This also helps in highlighting the importance of multiculturalism, tolerance, and inclusivity.

Conclusion

Singapore policymakers must remain vigilant in upholding the principles of multiculturalism. Policies that promote social cohesion, protect minority rights, and encourage intercultural dialogue are essential. Policymakers should consider the potential impact of transnational ideologies on the social fabric and proactively address any signs of exclusion within the society.

Endnotes

1. C. Jaffrelot and I. Therwath, "The Sangh Parivar and the Hindu diaspora in the West: What kind of 'long-distance nationalism'?" *International Political Sociology*, 1(3), 278–295 (2007). https://doi.org/10.1111/j.1749-5687.2007.00017.x.
2. *Ibid.*
3. The Indian population in Singapore is diverse, comprising various ethnicities, languages, and cultural practices. While Tamil is the most widely spoken language among the Indian community, other languages such as Hindi, Bengali, Punjabi, and Urdu are also represented. This diversity reflects the complex historical migration patterns and the presence of different Indian communities, including Tamils, Punjabis, Gujaratis, Malayalis, Telugus, and Sindhis. See S. Arasaratnam, *Indians in Malaysia and Singapore* (London: Institute of Race Relations, 2007; Originally Published 1970). See also, A. Lele, Hindutva and Singapore Confucianism as projects of political legitimation. Master's Theses/PhD Dissertation, Cornell University. https://hcommons.org/deposits/item/hc:19307/.
4. S. S. Amrith, *Migration and Diaspora in Modern Asia* (London, UK: Cambridge University Press, 2011). https://doi.org/10.1017/CBO9780511976346.
5. D. Reddy, "Hindutva as praxis", in *Religion Compass*, Vol. 5–8 (USA: Blackwell Publishing Ltd., 2011). https://doi.org/10.1111/j.1749-8171.2011.00288.x.
6. M. Vaishnav, "The BJP in power: Indian Democracy and religious nationalism", *Carnegie Endowment for International Peace*, April 4, 2019. https://carnegieendowment.org/research/2019/04/the-bjp-in-power-indian-democracy-and-religious-nationalism?lang=en.
7. C. Antara, "Hindu nationalism: Impact on multicultural societies", *RSIS Commentary*, March 7, 2023. https://www.rsis.edu.sg/rsis-publication/cens/hindu-nationalism-impact-on-multicultural-societies/.
8. Here, "Hindu" refers to a specific assertive strand of Hinduism promoted by the proponents of Hindu nationalism. This form of Hinduism emphasises a muscular and exclusive identity, often aligned with the political and ideological goals of Hindutva, as opposed to the more pluralistic and inclusive interpretations of Hindu tradition.
9. D. Reddy, "Capturing Hindutva: Rhetorics and strategies", *Religion Compass*, August 1, 2011, https://doi.org/10.1111/j.1749-8171.2011.00289.x.
10. S. Sarka, "Religion is keeping Indians apart, especially in the north of the country: Pew", *South China Morning Post*, July 6, 2021. https://www.scmp.com/week-asia/politics/article/3140048/religion-keeping-indians-apart-especially-north-country-pew.
11. G. Kuthar, "The slow, steady march of Hindutva in South India", *Frontline*, July 6, 2024. https://frontline.thehindu.com/columns/south-india-bjp-win-thrissur-vote-share-increase-tamil-nadu-andhra-pradesh-telangana-lok-sabha/article68340247.ece.
12. Antara (2023). *Op. cit.*

13. U. Swadźba, "The impact of globalization on the traditional value system", in *The Scale of Globalization. Think Globally, Act Locally, Change Individually in the 21st Century* (Poland: University of Ostrava, 2011), pp. 332–37. https://globalization.osu.cz/publ2011/332-337_Swadzba.pdf.
14. A. Truschke, "Hindutva's dangerous rewriting of history", *South Asia Multidisciplinary Academic Journal*, 24/25, December 14, 2020. https://doi.org/10.4000/samaj.6636.
15. Vaishnav (2019). *Op. cit.*
16. *Ibid.*
17. L. Varma, "Ram temple event fervour across the globe: Yatras, rallies, and bhajans from New York to Sydney", *Indian Express*, January 14, 2024. https://indianexpress.com/article/political-pulse/ram-temple-event-fervour-across-the-globe-9108036/.
18. VHP Thailand. 2024. "On the occasion of the historical event of the Ram Janmabhoomi, VHP Thailand, in collaboration with Dev Mandir and Hindu Samaj Bangkok, is celebrating the event on January 22, 2024, at Dev Mandir Bangkok, graced by H.E. Mr. Nagesh Singh, Ambassador and PR to UNESCAP, Embassy of India." *X (formerly Twitter)*. January 10, 2024. https://x.com/vhpthailand/status/1745303581845254600.
19. *Ibid.*
20. PTI, "Singapore Indians to host cultural evening for PM Modi", *The Economic Times*, November 14, 2015. https://economictimes.indiatimes.com/news/politics-and-nation/singapore-indians-to-host-cultural-evening-for-pm-modi/articleshow/49778680.cms?from=mdr.
21. R. Velloor, "India's Prime Minister Narendra Modi is The Straits Times Asian of the Year 2014", *The Straits Times*, January 19, 2016. https://www.straitstimes.com/asia/south-asia/indias-prime-minister-narendra-modi-is-the-straits-times-asian-of-the-year-2014.
22. P. Mallick, "Diaspora Hinduism and Hindutva: A historiography of modern Indian politics", in S. Raudino and P. Sohn (eds.) *Beyond the Death of God: Religion in 21st Century International Politics* (USA: University of Michigan Press, 2022), pp. 314–36. http://www.jstor.org/stable/10.3998/mpub.11866503.19.
23. M. J. Dutta, "Digital platforms, Hindutva, and disinformation: Communicative strategies and the leicester violence", *Communication Monographs* (April), 1–29 (2024). https://doi.org/10.1080/03637751.2024.2339799.
24. S. Tadepalli and S. Viswanat, "How 'Hinduphobia' is being weaponised in the US", *Scroll.in*, January 7, 2024. https://scroll.in/article/1060250/how-hinduphobia-is-being-weaponised-in-the-us.
25. The Hindu Staff, "Social media influencers are India's new election campaigners", March 27, 2024. https://www.thehindu.com/sci-tech/technology/social-media-influencers-are-indias-new-election-campaigners/article67996976.ece.
26. Mallick (2022). *Op. cit.*

27. N. Onishi and I. Vjosa, "Modi's Hindu nationalism Stokes tension in Indian diaspora", *The New York Times*, September 30, 2023. https://www.nytimes.com/2023/09/30/world/canada/modi-canada-hindu-nationalism.html.
28. D. P. S Goh, "Diversity and nation-building in Singapore", *Global Centre for Pluralism*, 2017. https://www.pluralism.ca/wp-content/uploads/2017/10/Singapore_EN.pdf.
29. "Racial and religious harmony circles", n.d. https://www.harmonycircle.sg/.
30. "The International Conference on Cohesive Societies", n.d. https://www.iccs.sg/.
31. OnePeople.Sg. (n.d.). About Us. OnePeople.Sg. https://www.onepeople.sg/about-us.
32. W. Miner, "In Singapore, religious diversity and tolerance go hand in hand", *Pew Research Center*, October 6, 2023. https://www.pewresearch.org/short-reads/2023/10/06/in-singapore-religious-diversity-and-tolerance-go-hand-in-hand/#:~:text=Followers%20of%20all%20faiths%20in,is%20the%20only%20true%20religion.
33. Chakraborthy(2023). *Op. cit.*
34. *Ibid.*
35. Ministry of Home Affairs, "Maintaining racial and religious harmony", n.d. https://www.mha.gov.sg/what-we-do/managing-security-threats/maintaining-racial-and-religious-harmony.
36. E. Leidig, "Reconfiguring nationalism: Transnational entanglements of Hindutva and radical right ideology", PhD Dissertation, Tilburg University, 2020. https://pure.uvt.nl/ws/portalfiles/portal/75910870/PhD-Leidig-2020.pdf.
37. C. Soon, N. B. Krishnan, and S. Goh, "Targeted approach needed to boost digital literacy", *The Straits Times*, June 22, 2022. https://www.straitstimes.com/opinion/targeted-approach-needed-to-boost-digital-literacy.
38. United Nations Sustainable Development Group, "UN resilience guidance: Executive summary", September 2021. https://unsdg.un.org/sites/default/files/2021-09/UN-Resilience-Guidance-Exec-Summ-Sept.pdf.
39. A. Chakraborthy, "Hindutva's rise and social cohesion", *RSIS Commentary*, February 8, 2022. https://www.rsis.edu.sg/rsis-publication/rsis/hindutvas-rise-and-social-cohesion/.
40. S. Arasaratnam, "Indians in Malaysia and Singapore" (London: Institute of Race Relations, 2007; Originally Published 1970).
41. A. Chakraborthy, "Hindu Nationalism's impact on multicultural societies", *RSIS Commentary*, March 7, 2023. https://www.rsis.edu.sg/rsis-publication/cens/hindu-nationalism-impact-on-multicultural-societies/.

PART 3

WOKE MOVEMENT

© 2025 Nanyang Technological University
https://doi.org/10.1142/9789819812691_0006

CHAPTER 6

The Implications of the Woke and Anti-Woke Movements on Social Cohesion

Yasmine Wong

Key Points
- The universality and adaptability of "wokeness" has resulted in its prevalence among youth both within and beyond Singapore.
- "Wokeness", resulting in extreme ideas and behaviours from the left, has led to a pushback from the right.
- Wokeness has been blamed for divisiveness within Western societies both because of its alienation of moderate and centrist segments of the population and the judgemental attitudes held against those who may not share the same views.
- It is not inconceivable that a conflict between woke and anti-woke camps occurs in Singapore, adversely affecting the city-state's social cohesion.
- There is an urgent need to reconcile both sides, before they stray to either extreme and consensus becomes impossible to achieve.

Introduction

"Woke" – a term which originated from Black communities within the racial justice movements in the early to mid-1900s[1] – has since been popularised on a global scale and has made it into the vocabulary of everyday conversations and political debates. To be "woke" is, generally, to be well informed on societal injustices and inequalities.

Although "wokeness" is seen as a Western phenomenon, the universality and adaptability of "wokeness" have resulted in its prevalence among the global youth, including those in Singapore.[2]

In the West, wokeness has become a "lightning rod on both the left and the right", symbolising the emergence of a "modern culture war".[3] As "wokeness" invariably results in extreme ideas and behaviours from the left, there has been a resultant pushback from the right as seen by the rise of anti-woke movements in the West[4] as well as Asia.[5] This phenomenon can be understood as two sides of the same coin, as both have resulted in mutual radicalisation. In countries like the US, and Europe, the conflict between woke and anti-woke camps has led to the rise of "culture wars", and thus social polarisation, dealing indelible consequences on social cohesion.[6]

It is not inconceivable that a conflict between woke and anti-woke camps occurs in Singapore, especially over sensitive issues like LGBTQ+, race, religion, and even gender, adversely affecting the city-state's social cohesion.

Wokeness, the Weaponisation of Cancel Culture, and Stifling Societal Debates

At its core, "wokeness" postulates that there is pervasive "oppression based on race, gender, sexual preference, disability, body size and other identities" in modern liberal societies, which requires a "social justice revolution" as a solution to dismantle the discrimination.[7] This requires the constant examination of societal interactions for potential biases and inequalities.[8]

Beyond Western contexts, the universality and ambiguity of the term "woke" contribute to its appeal, making it easily adaptable across the world, where the term applies to being aware of systems of oppression and inequality specific to contextual conditions. The connectedness of youths to global public spaces via the Internet has also facilitated the transmission of social justice movements like Black Lives Matter and MeToo, which have since been glocalised to reflect local instances of discrimination.[9]

Some have argued that wokeness makes the practice of public life extremely challenging.[10] The woke "instinct", when put into practice, has been blamed for the shutting down of debate surrounding contentious issues. Rather than prompting action, wokeness may end up stifling social justice work, because social problems are portrayed to be massively pervasive and intractable.[11]

There are also parallel concerns about woke culture's potential focus on political correctness, which may overshadow the main work of dismantling social injustices. As American journalist Nellie Bowles observes, "When the area around a child is very well disinfected, her immune system will keep searching for a fight".[12]

Furthermore, the weaponising of cancel culture[13] by woke proponents – that is, taking away people's jobs or social standing because of a statement, action, behaviour, or speech considered to be bigoted[14] – has stymied debate over important and sensitive issues. Some debates on trans rights and gender reflect this very outcome. For instance, trans activists have been campaigning to have their rights recognised, whether it is the abolishment of "demeaning" medical checks before recognition of a change in legal sex[15] or gender-neutral bathrooms. While cancel culture has helped to problematise transphobic narratives in public spaces, others have also raised concerns that women who are expressing legitimate fears about what this means for them in private spaces, and whether it will affect their access to services like domestic violence shelters, are being shut down.[16]

Some have raised the argument that cancel culture can be good for society in terms of holding individuals/groups to account. For instance, the MeToo movement started off as a reckoning for many powerful figures in Hollywood, where many offenders were "cancelled".[17] This soon became a social movement that spread globally[18] and sparked public conversations about sexual assault and harassment. In this case, "cancelling" not only articulated a community's consensus on acceptable behaviour, contributing to progressive norm building, but also enabled victims to obtain justice.

On the other hand, cancel culture has sparked concerns due to its impact on everyday citizens who may not be as resourceful at navigating being cancelled as someone in a powerful position.[19] Although it can give a voice/recourse to victims, it also means that those identified/perceived as "guilty" may not have the opportunity to defend themselves, turning the judicial process on its head.[20] Furthermore, some have called into question the "collectives" in cancel culture and whether the consensus built in instances of cancelling is but a form of mob mentality.[21]

Emergence of Anti-Woke Movements and Their Use of Cancel Culture

Wokeness has been blamed for divisiveness within Western societies both because of its alienation of moderate and centrist segments of the population and the judgemental attitudes held against those who may not share the same views.[22] When taken to the extreme, this has banished some from the conversation and has led to a rift in the Left. The implication within the Woke movement that those who are not subscribed to it are wrong, forms a dividing line with this judgment, stalling the debate and "forcing the other side to become defensive".[23]

Although wokeness is seen as a problem of the left, any analysis of wokeness would be remiss if it omits discussion of the anti-woke movements of the right. "Woke" has increasingly become a rallying point for the right (and far right), with assaults on "political correctness" and the liberal left normalising far-right presence in mainstream politics in the West.[24] This has resulted in "a debate between global liberalism and anti-liberal, traditionalist ideas".[25]

As mentioned earlier, "wokeness" is an all-encompassing catchphrase for a "wide variety of social movements" concerning "LGBT rights, feminism, immigration, climate change and marginalised communities".[26] As such, attacks on "wokeness" encompass backlash not just against the more "extreme" expressions of wokeness but also against any movement that aims at greater parity for minorities and other disadvantaged groups.[27] Anti-wokeness – an ideology in itself – is as such a mere rebrand of bigotry.[28]

Across Asia, Western anti-woke personalities like Andrew Tate have managed to amass a following, with boys and young men particularly susceptible to anti-woke recruitment.[29] This engagement is amplified by social media algorithms that disproportionately recommend anti-woke content to boys and young men.[30] Initial interest in conservatism, combined with algorithms pushing more extreme content, has given rise to the phenomenon of Asian users being "influenced online" by "far-right causes".[31]

Local conservative figures in Southeast Asia have also capitalised on the rhetoric that "progressive" values and movements (e.g., LGBTQ+

and feminist movements) are alien to the region and have been imported from the West.[32] While this is an ahistorical claim in Asia, where issues of sexuality are not new and hail back to pre-colonial times, the dominance of this narrative highlights the strong East-versus-West narrative in conversations on "wokeness" in Asia[33]. This overshadows and delegitimises grassroots efforts to improve societal conditions. Conservative groups in Southeast Asia have also engaged in acts of "cancelling". In Malaysia and Indonesia, conservative Muslim groups Perkasa[34] and Muhammadiyah[35] joined together to boycott Starbucks in 2017 over its support of gay rights.[36]

Extremism From Far Left to Far Right

In the West, instances of the conservative right and far right cancelling those on the left have been observed.[37] For instance, book-banning efforts across the US among the right reveal a similar phenomenon, where, for instance, Moms for Liberty, a right-wing advocacy group, tried to get books banned from Tennessee schools because they contained content they perceived to be disturbing. Examples include books on Galileo being anti-church.[38] A "vitriolic and violent alt-right" and an "'unhinged' left", as Angela Nagle describes, have come head-to-head in what has come to be known as "culture wars".[39] Culture wars have resulted in the ideological polarisation of not only Western politics but also the public.[40] While the American public may be less ideologically polarised than they perceive themselves to be, one cannot neglect the high levels of "emotional polarisation".[41] This intense mutual dislike of the other side has eaten away at political compromise or the ability to establish consensus – an essential part of public life.

Within this ecosystem of wokeness and anti-wokeness, the two sides are trapped in a cycle of mutual radicalisation, where extreme actions undertaken by one side are reciprocated in equal measure by the other.[42] This solidifies the two camps in their hatred towards one another, pushing the populace to the extreme ends, further thinning out the middle ground.

The Woke Movement in Singapore

In Singapore, "wokeness" is not clearly defined. It encompasses a wide range of social justice issues and has been used to describe anything from a liberal outlook[43] to the rise of new issues and fault lines inspired by similar movements in the West (e.g., issues surrounding gender identity).[44] It also encapsulates the push for greater "political correctness" in public spaces and has been used to describe the phenomenon of youths in Singapore who are keyed into and are passionate about social issues.[45]

Concerns over wokeness and the use of cancel culture have been expressed. For instance, former Singapore Prime Minister Lee Hsien Loong remarked in a recent interview that wokeness makes life "very burdensome".[46] This burden derives from being "super-sensitive about other people's issues" and hypersensitive when one perceives disrespect to oneself or one's super-subgroup, which does not make for constructive dialogue and can undermine resilience and cohesiveness in society.[47]

A case in point was the repeal of Section 377A and the debates that predated and followed the repeal. During the parliamentary debate on the repeal, members of parliament from both the ruling and opposition parties expressed concerns over the divisiveness of LGBTQ+ issues, stating that tensions could lead to a rise in cancel culture.[48] At the heart of these concerns was the expected clash of worldviews between supporters of LGBTQ+ issues and their critics and the use of cancel culture to enforce more liberal societal norms surrounding issues of sexuality.[49]

Nevertheless, the woke movement and cancel culture in Singapore are not as prevalent in public discourse as in the West, and studies in Singapore indicate "low levels of political polarisation".[50]

However, if the woke movement and cancel culture gain traction and momentum, it is likely that there will be a pushback from an anti-woke movement, which could undermine social cohesion as observable in other countries. Furthermore, "wokeness" (and progressiveness) and the movements that have risen in its counter have already exposed divisions where these issues have proved polarising. These intersect fault lines like age, gender, and religion. The rise of "anti-woke" culture, especially among boys and young men across the region, also points to the evolution of the "woke problem", with the growth of a potentially susceptible audience for far-right narratives.[51]

Conclusion

There are questions being raised about the reality of wokeness as a passing fad, with a discourse on the genuineness of woke culture – now capitalised upon by big businesses[52] – and trends that indicate a swing towards dismantling wokeness and anti-wokeness. In an opinion piece, Michelle Goldberg remarked that though there are regrettable aspects of woke culture that she is happy to see go, the movement in general represented a "rare moment" imbued with a sudden surge of "societal energy to tackle long-festering inequalities".[53]

Whilst challenging, progressiveness and the more unsavoury strands of "wokeness" should not be conflated, especially amidst shifting norms in Singapore. The extension of explicit protection to the LGBTQ+ community against violence incited by conservative and/or religious groups or movements in the Maintenance of Religious Harmony Act (MRHA)[54] and the repeal of Section 377A reflect steps taken by

Singapore's society towards the normalisation and recognition of LGBTQ+ issues. Amidst this progressive shift, there is an urgent need to reconcile both sides before they stray to either extreme and consensus becomes impossible to achieve.

Endnotes

1. K. Alfonseca, "What does 'woke' mean and why are some conservatives using it?", *ABC News*, January 24, 2024. https://abcnews.go.com/Politics/woke-conservatives/story?id=93051138.
2. "Too much of 'wokeism' can become too much of a good thing", *The Straits Times*, January 10, 2021. https://www.straitstimes.com/opinion/too-much-of-wokeism-can-become-too-much-of-a-good-thing.
3. J. Luk, "Why 'woke' became toxic", *Al Jazeera*, June 24, 2021, https://www.aljazeera.com/opinions/2021/6/24/what-is-woke-culture-and-why-has-it-become-so-toxic.
4. M. Harriot, "War on wokeness: The year the right rallied around a made-up menace", *The Guardian*, December 21, 2022. https://www.theguardian.com/us-news/2022/dec/20/anti-woke-race-america-history.
5. B. Wood and J. Tse, "Divided youth: 'Anti-woke' movement recruits teen boys across Asia", *South China Morning Post*, July 22, 2024. https://www.scmp.com/video/asia/3270920/divided-youth-anti-woke-movement-recruits-teen-boys-across-asia.
6. B. Bowman, "'A country on fire': New poll finds America polarized over culture, race and 'woke'", *NBC News*, April 27, 2023. https://www.nbcnews.com/meet-the-press/first-read/-country-fire-new-poll-finds-america-polarized-culture-race-woke-rcna81592.
7. C. Young, "The pushback against 'wokeness' is legitimate", *CATO Institute*, June 8, 2023. https://www.cato.org/commentary/pushback-against-wokeness-legitimate.
8. *Ibid.*
9. N. Vasu and Y. Wong, "BLM movement: Singapore and glocalisation", *RSIS Commentaries*, July 13, 2020. https://www.rsis.edu.sg/rsis-publication/CENS/BLM-MOVEMENT-SINGAPORE-AND-GLOCALISATION/.
10. D. Brooks, "The problem with wokeness", *The New York Times*, June 7, 2018. https://www.nytimes.com/2018/06/07/opinion/wokeness-racism-progressivism-social-justice.html.
11. *Ibid.*
12. M. Goldberg, "Wokeness is dying. We might miss it", *The New York Times*, May 17, 2024. https://www.nytimes.com/2024/05/17/opinion/wokeness-is-dying-we-might-miss-it.html.

13. Cancel culture is the glossier term referring to the act of "collective boycott" at perceived wrongdoing, now a bigger phenomenon than ever because of the affordances of social media, cancel culture, akin to acts of public shaming. This has been used as a deplatforming tool to hold individuals in power responsible for their actions – something traditional institutions may fail to do. See M. Lo-Booth, "What is cancel culture and what does it mean in 2024?", *VICE*, March 14, 2024. https://www.vice.com/en/article/dy35jm/cancel-culture-meaning.
14. G. Poonia, "The true meaning of the 'woke mob'", *Deseret News*, January 25, 2023. https://www.deseret.com/2022/9/10/23307085/woke-mob-meaning/.
15. J. Luk, "Why 'woke' became toxic", *Al Jazeera*, June 24, 2021. https://www.aljazeera.com/opinions/2021/6/24/what-is-woke-culture-and-why-has-it-become-so-toxic.
16. *Ibid.*
17. "Five years on, how #MeToo shook the world", *The Straits Times*, October 7, 2022. https://www.straitstimes.com/world/united-states/five-years-on-how-metoo-shook-the-world.
18. In the Philippines, a study by milieu showed that 1 in 5 Filipinos has participated in moves to cancel a person or group, with the majority surveyed believing that cancel culture is a tool to demand responsibility. See Y. Marquez, "Is cancel culture doing more harm than good in the Philippines?" *milieu*, September 15, 2022. https://www.mili.eu/sg/insights/is-cancel-culture-doing-more-harm-than-good-in-the-philippines.
19. Lo-Booth (2024). *Op. cit.*
20. S. Decker, "#METOO and cancel culture", *2010s Project*, n.d. https://2010sproject metoo.carrd.co/.
21. E. A. Vogels, M. Anderson, M. Porteus, C. Baronavski, S. Atske, C. McClain, B. Auxier, A. Perrin, and M. Ramshankar, "Americans and 'cancel culture': Where some see calls for accountability, others see censorship, punishment", *Pew Research Center,* May 19, 2021. https://www.pewresearch.org/internet/2021/05/19/americans-and-cancel-culture-where-some-see-calls-for-accountability-others-see-censorship-punishment/.
22. J. Luk, "Why 'woke' became toxic", *Al Jazeera*, June 24, 2021. https://www.aljazeera.com/opinions/2021/6/24/what-is-woke-culture-and-why-has-it-become-so-toxic.
23. *Ibid.*
24. Lundius (2024). *Op. cit.*
25. I. Kazazis, "The creeping ascent of the far-right in mainstream European politics and how to stop it", *LSE Blogs*, February 6, 2024. https://blogs.lse.ac.uk/lseupr/2024/02/06/the-creeping-ascent-of-the-far-right-in-mainstream-european-politics-and-how-to-stop-it/.
26. J. Lundius, "Is anti-woke a grass-root movement?", *Global Issues,* February 8, 2024. https://www.globalissues.org/news/2024/02/08/35946; Alfonseca (2024). *Op. cit.*

27. S. C. Fanjul, "Why wokeness has pitched the left into crisis", *El Pais,* March 11, 2024. https://english.elpais.com/international/2024-03-11/why-wokeness-has-pitched-the-left-into-crisis.html; Alfonseca (2024). *Op. cit.*
28. M. Harriot, "War on wokeness: the year the right rallied around a made-up menace", *The Guardian,* December 21, 2022. https://www.theguardian.com/us-news/2022/dec/20/anti-woke-race-america-history.
29. B. Wood and J. Tse, "Divided youth: 'Anti-woke' movement recruits teen boys across Asia", *South China Morning Post,* July 22, 2024. https://www.scmp.com/video/asia/3270920/divided-youth-anti-woke-movement-recruits-teen-boys-across-asia.
30. S. Weale, "Social media algorithms 'amplifying misogynistic content'", *The Guardian,* February 6, 2024. https://www.theguardian.com/media/2024/feb/06/social-media-algorithms-amplifying-misogynistic-content.
31. K. Lim, "Far-right views in Southeast Asia? How 2 Singapore cases may reflect 'anti-woke' movement's slow creep", *South China Morning Post,* February 17, 2024. https://www.scmp.com/week-asia/people/article/3252233/far-right-views-southeast-asia-how-2-singapore-cases-may-reflect-anti-woke-movements-slow-creep.
32. *Ibid.*
33. *Ibid.*
34. A prominent Muslim group with about 700,000 members.
35. Indonesia's second-largest Muslim group.
36. "Malaysia Muslim group joins Indonesian call for Starbucks boycott over LGBT stand", *The Straits Times,* July 7, 2017. https://www.straitstimes.com/asia/se-asia/malaysia-muslim-group-joins-indonesian-call-for-starbucks-boycott-over-lgbt-stand.
37. A. Mahawi, "Cancel culture is real but it's not the 'woke mob' you should worry about", *The Guardian,* February 1, 2022. https://www.theguardian.com/commentisfree/2022/feb/01/cancel-culture-books-anti-church-lgbtq-banned-us'; Wil Del Pilar, "Even While Railing Against It, the Republican Party Has Become a Champion of Cancel Culture", *US News,* 24 July 2024, https://www.usnews.com/opinion/articles/2024-07-24/even-while-railing-against-it-the-republican-party-has-become-a-champion-of-cancel-culture; Steve Israel, "The cancel culture of the right", *The Hill,* 16 February 2022, https://thehill.com/opinion/civil-rights/594423-the-cancel-culture-of-the-right/.
38. *Ibid.*
39. F. Sobanda, A. Kanai, and N. Zeng, "The hypervisibility and discourses of 'wokeness' in digital culture", *Media, Culture & Society,* 44(8) (2022).
40. R. Kleinfeld, "Polarization, democracy, and political violence in the United States: What the research says", *Carnegie Endowment for Peace,* September 5, 2023. https://carnegieendowment.org/research/2023/09/polarization-democracy-and-political-violence-in-the-united-states-what-the-research-says?lang=en.
41. Emotional polarisation (or affective polarisation) refers to a strong dislike of the other side. See: Kleinfeld (2023). *Op. cit.*

42. F. M. Moghaddam, "Introduction" in *Mutual Radicalization: How Groups and Nations Drive Each Other to Extremes* (American Psychological Association, 2018).
43. D. Tham, "Are young women more 'woke' than their male peers? In Singapore, it's not so clear-cut", *Channel News Asia*, February 9, 2024. https://www.channelnewsasia.com/singapore/gender-gap-politics-ideology-woke-left-right-conservative-liberal-gen-z-4110016.
44. D. Osman, "Don't let gender identity issues divide Singapore's society: Lawrence Wong", *Yahoo News*, February 1, 2021. https://sg.news.yahoo.com/do-not-let-gender-identity-issues-divide-society-lawrence-wong-061642799.html.
45. J. Ong, "Youth passion on social issues is positive, but patience is key to societal changes: Sim Ann", *The Straits Times*, July 24, 2021. https://www.straitstimes.com/singapore/youth-passion-on-social-issues-is-positive-but-patience-is-key-to-societal-changes-sim-ann; J. Theseira, "Unfazed by upheaval, more young S'poreans are woke with hope", *The Straits Times*, December 21, 2021. https://www.straitstimes.com/singapore/unfazed-by-upheaval-more-young-sporeans-are-woke-with-hope.
46. T. Suresh, "'Can we elect him Prime Minister here, please?': PM Lee's take on 'wokeness' praised by Australian media", *Mothership*, May 15, 2024. https://mothership.sg/2024/05/pm-lee-wokeness-comments-australian-tv/. "Wokeness movement makes life 'very burdensome': PM Lee", *CNA*, May 11, 2024. Available at: https://www.youtube.com/watch?v=3LdabP7FLjE.
47. *Ibid.*
48. J. Lau, "MPs raise concerns over cancel culture in discussion of LGBT issues", *The Straits Times*, November 28, 2022. https://www.straitstimes.com/singapore/politics/mps-raise-concerns-over-cancel-culture-in-discussion-of-lgbt-issues.
49. *Ibid.*
50. J. Ong, "Singapore perspectives conference: S'pore not beset by political polarisation, but class, culture divides a concern: Panellists", *The Straits Times*, January 19, 2021. https://www.straitstimes.com/singapore/politics/singapore-perspectives-conference-spore-not-beset-by-political-polarisation-but.
51. Y. Wong, "Misogyny and violent extremism – A potential national security issue", *RSIS Commentary*, September 23, 2024. https://www.rsis.edu.sg/rsis-publication/rsis/misogyny-and-violent-extremism-a-potential-national-security-issue/.
52. A. White, "DEI initiatives are dissolving — Here's how managers can step up and reverse this unsettling trend", *Entrepreneur*, January 11, 2024. https://www.entrepreneur.com/growing-a-business/dei-initiatives-are-dissolving-how-leaders-can-reverse/465726.
53. M. Goldbert, "Wokeness is dying. We might miss it", *New York Times*, May 17, 2024. https://www.nytimes.com/2024/05/17/opinion/wokeness-is-dying-we-might-miss-it.html.
54. N. Elangovan, "New legislation protects LGBTQ community from religiously motivated violence but law is 'same for all'", *Today*, October 15, 2019. https://www.todayonline.com/singapore/new-legislation-protects-lgbtq-community-religiously-motivated-violence-law-same-all.

PART 4

ENVIRONMENTAL/CLIMATE ACTIVISM

CHAPTER 7

Environmental/Climate Activism and Youth: An Update*

Margareth Sembiring

Key Points
- Since the 1960s, youth have been at the forefront of environmental advocacy, with environmental education serving as a catalyst for action.
- In parts of Southeast Asia, youth environmentalism often gives voice to broader social justice and human rights issues.
- The appeal of Greta Thunberg's Fridays for Future (FFF) movement lies in its role as an expression of youth dissent and an avenue to exercise agency to critique power relations and political interests that underlie environmental issues.
- While youth-led environmentalism encapsulates a positive force for change, various beliefs and approaches to climate change can potentially challenge national cohesion.
- Environmental activism often capitalises on fear and alarmist narratives to garner support and push for stronger pro-environmental action. The intensity of alarmist messages is likely to increase in the coming years.

*The author declares the use of an AI tool.

Introduction

Youth involvement in environmental movements dates back to the 1960s. Catalysed by environmental education and the growing awareness of environmental problems, millions of young people across the United States participated in the first Earth Day in 1970, with about fifteen hundred colleges and ten thousand schools being involved in teach-ins.[1] This signified a pivotal moment for youth involvement in environmental movements and gave rise to what is called the first Green Generation.[2]

Youth-led environmentalism focused on a wide range of issues, depending on the unique socio-cultural, economic, and political contexts the youth find themselves in. From a bamboo bicycle project in Ghana to swimming lessons for emergencies in Bangladesh to building cyclone-proof schools in Madagascar,[3] most of their activities are aimed at capacity building and raising awareness at the local level. In addition to their involvement in initiatives like community gardens, tree planting, river clean-ups, and wildlife habitat restoration, they also actively engage their peers and the broader community on issues such as urban pollution, deforestation, and biodiversity conservation.

In more specific contexts, youth environmentalism can extend to more persuasive actions. In Sweden, youth have been participating in demonstrations and strikes since the 1970s.[4] In the United States, the youth-led Sunrise Movement successfully advocated for the adoption of the Green New Deal during the Biden administration (2021–2024).[5]

In parts of Southeast Asia, youth environmentalism often gives voice to broader social justice and human rights issues. Environmental advocacy is often integrated within larger struggles against inequality and support for indigenous rights and labour rights. The linkage between environmental concerns and social justice indeed presents a strong appeal for youth support and activism.[6] For example, the Indonesian environmental youth group Jaga Rimba ("Protect Forest") founded by 15-year-old Salsabila Khairunissa actively advocates for the protection of the land rights of the Laman Kinipan indigenous community in the Central Kalimantan Province, who are disproportionately affected by the expansion of palm oil plantations in the area.[7]

The importance of embracing young people is widely acknowledged at the global level. The inclusive approach is evident in various youth-focused groupings established under formal institutions and processes, including the United Nations Framework Convention on Climate Change (UNFCCC). Since 2009, the UNFCCC has welcomed children and youth in its processes through its YOUNGO constituency.[8] YOUNGO not only facilitates interactions between various youth environmental groups from different parts of the world but also grants them a voice at international climate conferences. For instance, in 2015, a representative from the Singapore Youth for Climate Action delivered a speech on behalf of YOUNGO at the UNFCCC COP21 in Paris.[9]

The Fridays for Future (FFF) Movement Has a Global Reach

While youth have been actively involved in environmental causes for over fifty years, the launch of the Fridays for Future (FFF) movement by Greta Thunberg in 2018 marked a significant shift in youth-led environmentalism.[10] Her skipping school for a solitary climate strike outside the Swedish Parliament was a novel tactic that deeply resonated with the youth and unprecedentedly mobilised millions worldwide at a remarkable scale and speed. Thunberg's FFF movement strengthened the sense of solidarity, common purpose, and personal values on climate change among young people,[11] which powerfully drove the formulation of their collective identity.[12]

Another compelling factor is eco-anxiety, which refers to the deep anxiety about climate impacts that can affect emotional, psychological, and spiritual health,[13] especially of vulnerable groups including the youth.[14] Fears over the looming threat of climate change drive young people to seek ways to actively address the issue. This is evidenced in youth-led environmentalism's increasing focus on climate change in tandem with growing scientific evidence, international policy, and global awareness.

Beyond collective identity and solidarity, the FFF movement symbolises an expression of youth dissent and is an avenue for the youth to exercise their agency to critique power relations and political interests that underlie environmental issues.[15] This holds a strong appeal for the youth who often feel marginalised in political decision-making processes. For example, Australian youth have shown considerable willingness to join protests in support of environmental movements,[16] demonstrating their readiness to challenge the status quo. The FFF movement confronts fossil fuel interests and seeks to transform societal norms and economic policies, thus granting youth a sense of empowerment so that they can make a tangible difference in an issue area that is usually inaccessible to them.

The forging of bonds and connections among youth has been greatly facilitated by social media platforms like Twitter, Instagram, and TikTok. These platforms enable young activists to reach a large audience, form global networks, share resources, and coordinate actions across borders quickly and efficiently.[17]

This global reach has likewise exposed young environmental activists in Southeast Asia to the FFF movement. Inspired by it, they have amplified their voices, organised larger protests, and pushed for stronger action on climate change. In 2019, the city of Bangkok saw 200 young activists staging a strike at the Natural Resources and Environment Ministry.[18] That same year, hundreds of students and members of civil society organisations took to the streets of the Indonesian capital Jakarta.[19] In the Philippines, the Youth Advocates for Climate Action Philippines actively organised demonstrations[20] and staged Friday protests.[21] In Singapore, a group of university students launched an online strike to express their views and demand stronger climate action.[22] Similarly, the Indonesian Jaga Rimba youth protesters skipped school to stage a protest in front of the Ministry of Environment and Forestry in early 2020.[23]

Potential Challenges to Social Cohesion

While youth-led environmentalism encapsulates a positive force for change, various beliefs and approaches to climate change within society can potentially challenge national cohesion. For instance, the climate change issue has deeply polarised American society in recent decades, mirroring the polarisation within US political parties.[24,25] Similarly, in Europe, although traditionally less pronounced compared to the US,[26] polarisation over climate change issues has increasingly become more intense as evidenced by demonstrations by farmers in Belgium, France, Germany, the Netherlands, and Spain in early 2024.[27] In addition, on social media, differing views on climate change have led to a politically charged atmosphere,[28] created echo chamber effects, and further worsened polarisation.[29]

While such polarisation has yet to manifest in the same way in Southeast Asia, the experience in other regions points to the need to ensure constructive interactions between environmental activism and the varied responses within society at large. Governments and relevant stakeholders should be aware of the potential divisive consequences and should proactively facilitate inclusive dialogues among groups and individuals with different standpoints on environmental issues. Inclusivity is key, especially considering the different impacts that climate action and other environmental initiatives may have on different elements of society. For example, those working in the fossil fuel industry will be negatively impacted by anti-fossil fuel measures.

Balancing environmental stewardship and social cohesion necessitates an emphasis on compromise, common ground, and collaboration. Although the pace of progress may be slower, a collaborative approach that incorporates various perspectives from within the community is more likely to get stronger buy-in. A collaborative approach likewise mitigates the tendency to demonise individuals, groups, or institutions with differing responses to environmental challenges.

Beyond inclusive dialogues and collaboration, fostering cohesion can be facilitated by having a high awareness of society's changing attitudes towards climate and energy policy through annual surveys. Providing counselling and outreach services to individuals, including children and youth who experience eco-anxiety, can assist people in managing their fears while society takes collaborative measures to address climate change.

Way Forward

Environmental activism often capitalises on fear and alarmist narratives to garner support and demand stronger pro-environmental action. Considering the narrowing time window to limit the rise in global temperature to below 1.5°C by the end of the century and the continuously rising greenhouse gas emissions despite mitigation efforts, alarmist messages are likely to intensify in the coming years. Despite their scientific basis and reasonable effectiveness, it is important to recognise that alarmist narratives have the potential to generate anxiety, harden stances, and hinder open dialogue with those with differing views.

In view of this divisive potential, it is imperative to promote balanced messaging, inclusive dialogue, collaboration, and direct support for those affected by eco-anxiety to harness passion and energy for the environment while maintaining social cohesion moving forward.

Endnotes

1. "The history of earth day", *Earth Day*, n.d. https://www.earthday.org/history/.
2. A. Rome, "The genius of earth day", *Environmental History*, 15(2), 194–205 (2010).
3. United Nations Joint Framework Initiative on and Children, Youth and Climate Change, *Youth in Action on Climate Change: Inspirations from around the World* (Bonn: United Nations Joint Framework Initiative on Children, Youth and Climate Change, 2013). https://unfccc.int/resource/docs/publications/publication_youth_2013.pdf.
4. B. Lundberg and D. L. Heidenblad, "Greta Thunberg emerged from five decades of environmental youth activism in Sweden", *The Conversation*, November 4, 2021. http://theconversation.com/greta-thunberg-emerged-from-five-decades-of-environmental-youth-activism-in-sweden-171043.
5. "Green new deal", *Sunrise Movement*, n.d. https://www.sunrisemovement.org/green-new-deal/.
6. S. R. Fisher, "Life trajectories of youth committing to climate activism", *Environmental Education Research*, 22(2), 229–47, February 17, 2016. https://doi.org/10.1080/13504622.2015.1007337.
7. "Jaga Rimba (@jaga_rimba) • Instagram photos and videos", n.d. https://www.instagram.com/jaga_rimba/.
8. "YOUNGO | UNFCCC", n.d. https://unfccc.int/topics/action-for-climate-empowerment-children-and-youth/youth/youngo.
9. "Singapore youth delivers speech at Paris climate talks", *TODAY*, December 10, 2015. https://www.todayonline.com/singapore/singapore-youth-delivers-speech-paris-climate-talks.

10. S. Neas, A. Ward, and B. Bowman, "Young people's climate activism: A review of the literature", *Frontiers in Political Science*, 4, August 4, 2022. https://doi.org/10.3389/fpos.2022.940876.
11. H. Wallis and L. S. Loy, "What drives pro-environmental activism of young people? A survey study on the Fridays for future movement", *Journal of Environmental Psychology*, 74, 101581 (2021), April 1, 2021. https://doi.org/10.1016/j.jenvp.2021.101581.
12. *Ibid.*
13. S. E. L. Burke, A. V. Sanson, and J. Van Hoorn, "The psychological effects of climate change on children", *Current Psychiatry Reports*, 20(5), 35 (2018), April 11, 2018. https://doi.org/10.1007/s11920-018-0896-9.
14. Y. Coffey *et al.*, "Understanding eco-anxiety: A systematic scoping review of current literature and identified knowledge gaps", *The Journal of Climate Change and Health*, 3, 100047 (2021), August 1, 2021. https://doi.org/10.1016/j.joclim.2021.100047.
15. K. O'Brien, E. Selboe, and B. M. Hayward, "Exploring youth activism on climate change: Dutiful, disruptive, and dangerous dissent", *Ecology and Society*, 23(3) (2018). https://www.jstor.org/stable/26799169.
16. L. J. Saha, M. Print, and K. Edwards, "Report 2: Youth, Political Engagement and Voting", n.d. https://www.aec.gov.au/About_AEC/Publications/files/youth-study/youth_electoral_study_02.pdf.
17. S. Nasrin and D. R. Fisher, "Understanding collective identity in virtual spaces: A study of the youth climate movement", *American Behavioral Scientist*, 66(9), 1286–308 (2022), August 1, 2022. https://doi.org/10.1177/00027642211056257.
18. Bangkok Post Public Company Limited, "Young climate strikers 'drop dead' at Environment Ministry", *Bangkok Post*, September 20, 2019. https://www.bangkokpost.com/thailand/general/1754589/young-climate-strikers-drop-dead-at-environment-ministry.
19. The Jakarta Post, "Indonesian cities join global climate strike - Sat, September 21, 2019", *The Jakarta Post*, Accessed June 9, 2024. https://www.thejakartapost.com/news/2019/09/21/indonesian-cities-join-global-climate-strike.html.
20. "Youth advocates for climate action Philippines", *Youth Advocates for Climate Action Philippines*, June 23, 2023. https://yacap.org/.
21. C. Fonbuena, "Philippines' youth call for systemic change at climate protest", *The Guardian*, September 24, 2021. Section: Global development. https://www.theguardian.com/global-development/2021/sep/24/philippines-youth-call-for-systemic-change-at-climate-protest.
22. "Students take part in 'online strike' to lobby S'pore Govt to measure carbon emissions in absolute terms", March 16, 2019. https://mothership.sg/2019/03/nus-students-climate-action-virtual-campaign/.
23. "100 Women: Salsabila Khairunisa, Remaja Indonesia Penggerak 'Mogok Sekolah Untuk Hutan' - BBC News Indonesia", November 30, 2020. https://www.bbc.com/indonesia/majalah-55120379.

24. A. M. McCright and R. E. Dunlap, "The politicization of climate change and polarization in the American public's views of global warming, 2001–2010", *The Sociological Quarterly*, 52(2), 155–94 (2011), May 1, 2011. https://doi.org/10.1111/j.1533-8525.2011.01198.x.
25. E. Keith Smith, M. Julia Bognar, and A. P. Mayer, "Polarisation of climate and environmental attitudes in the United States, 1973–2022", *Npj Climate Action*, 3(1), 1–14, January 10, 2024. https://doi.org/10.1038/s44168-023-00074-1.
26. S. D. Fisher et al., "The politicisation of climate change attitudes in Europe", *Electoral Studies*, 79, 102499 (2022), October 1, 2022. https://doi.org/10.1016/j.electstud.2022.102499.
27. "Is there a silver lining to Europe's climate change turmoil?" February 26, 2024. https://carnegieendowment.org/research/2024/02/is-there-a-silver-lining-to-europes-climate-change-turmoil?lang=en&center=europe.
28. M. Falkenberg et al., "Growing polarization around climate change on social media", *Nature Climate Change*, 12(12), 1114–21 (2022). https://doi.org/10.1038/s41558-022-01527-x.
29. C. W. van Eck, B. C. Mulder, and S. van der Linden, "Echo chamber effects in the climate change blogosphere", *Environmental Communication*, 15(2), 145–52 (2021), February 17, 2021. https://doi.org/10.1080/17524032.2020.1861048.

CHAPTER 8

Generation Green: How Young Activists Are Shaping Singapore's Climate Future Part 1

Amanda Huan

Key Points
- Today, there is a diverse climate action ecosystem in Singapore which counts both groups and individuals as major players.
- The increased availability of sustainability-oriented majors and careers has also significantly enhanced the appeal of youth climate activism.
- The motivations driving youth climate activism in Singapore are multifaceted, rooted in both personal and collective concerns about the future.
- The primary aim of youth climate activism in Singapore is to effect change.
- For most youth climate action groups, the primary target audience is usually the government, followed by the general public and, at times, private sector entities as well.

Introduction

Youth climate activism in Singapore has emerged as a significant and enduring force; however, it faces its own set of challenges. While the Singapore government's recent efforts to expand engagement with youths in this area mark a positive step forward, the youth climate action scene in Singapore remains complex. As young activists seize the opportunities presented, it is crucial for them to learn how to engage constructively and effectively.

This article is divided into two parts. The first explores the youth climate activism landscape in Singapore and the second part discusses changes and their potential impact on social cohesion, emphasising the importance of thoughtful participation and mutual understanding.

Shifts in Activism: From Basic Environmental Conservation to Sophisticated Advocacy

In November 2023, the National Youth Council of Singapore announced that it was launching a panel for youths to help formulate government environmental policies. Named #GreenHacks, the year-long initiative will see youths working alongside government bodies to help in research and policy formulation.[1] The idea for the initiative came from Minister for Culture, Community and Youth Edwin Tong, who received feedback from several youths about their desire to engage in deeper conversations with policymakers.

This initiative by the government represents another milestone in youth climate change activism efforts in Singapore. Early youth initiatives focused on environmental conservation and awareness-raising activities such as "going green", recycling and reducing waste campaigns, and beach clean-ups. Over time, there has been a shift towards more sophisticated forms of involvement such as participation in international forums like the United Nations Climate Change conferences and the evaluation of governmental policies. Youth climate activists in Singapore have also become more vocal and organised, forming groups such as the SG Climate Rally and LepakInSG. Today, there is a diverse climate action ecosystem in Singapore which counts both groups and individuals as major players. The proliferation of youth climate groups in Singapore has been accelerated by both global transnational forces and the increased availability of "green" or sustainability-oriented career pathways.

Global Influences on Youth Climate Activism

The global nature of the climate movement means that local activism is often influenced by international figures and movements. Greta Thunberg, for instance, has been a significant source of inspiration for many young activists in Singapore. Her Fridays for Future school strike campaign, which sparked a global movement, resonated with Singaporean youth, galvanising them to organise their own strikes and rallies. In 2020, for instance, one 18-year-old youth posed for a series of photos at the building housing ExxonMobil's Singapore office, holding up signs that read "Planet over profit". Another youth held up a placard in public that read "SG is better than oil" and made a specific reference to the Fridays for Future movement.[2] In 2019, SG Climate Rally organised the first mass climate rally in Singapore at Hong Lim Park, which was attended by more than 2,000 attendees. SG Climate Rally then held a second in-person gathering in 2023.

The increased availability of sustainability-oriented majors and careers has also significantly enhanced the appeal of youth climate activism. Historically, few career paths focused on sustainability, and many young activists pursued climate activism independently of their university majors, which often were not related to the environment. This disconnect led many youths to drop out or cease their activism upon entering full-time employment, as balancing a career with activism became challenging. However, the rise of sustainability-focused majors and careers now allows youths to align their activism with their academic and professional pursuits. This synergy makes climate activism more attractive to young people as it now complements their areas of study and future career paths.

Why Are Youths Drawn to Climate Activism?

The motivations driving youth climate activism in Singapore are multifaceted, rooted in both personal and collective concerns about the future.

For many young activists, the urgency of climate change is deeply personal. A 2022 survey by TODAY found that the top three feelings mentioned by youths when thinking about climate change were fear, sadness, and hopelessness.[3] They recognise that the environmental challenges the world faces today will have a profound impact on their lifetimes, influencing everything from health to economic stability. This long-term perspective fuels a passionate commitment to advocating for meaningful change. At the same time, there is a palpable sense of frustration among young people who are well informed about climate issues yet perceive a lack of corresponding action. This sentiment is encapsulated in the following question: "Why do we know so much but do so little?" This frustration drives youth to seek avenues where they can make a tangible difference, moving beyond symbolic actions to more substantial and influential efforts.

While traditional activities like beach clean-ups are important, there is a growing desire to engage in efforts that influence policy, shape public discourse, and drive systemic change. Several youth activists I spoke to had their first forays into environmental activism when they participated in beach or forest clean-ups. Thereafter, these youths expressed a desire to do more, and many subsequently joined the various activities organised by multiple youth climate action groups in Singapore. These activities include organising campaigns to raise greater awareness about environmental issues in Singapore, conducting research, working on environmental impact assessments, and providing feedback to the government on their environmental policies. For instance, LepakInSG offers a range of activities for volunteers. Its Public Action initiative aims to improve public literacy of government policies by engaging members of the public in discussions on government publications such as the Singapore Green Plan 2030.[4] Additionally, its Food Sustainability initiative uses research to raise awareness among Singaporeans about food consumption behaviours and food sustainability in Singapore.[5]

Main Target Audiences for Youth Climate Activists

Many young activists are drawn to climate activism because it offers a sense of purpose and the potential for significant impact. The primary aim of youth climate activism in Singapore is to effect change, and for most youth climate action groups, the primary target audience is usually the government, followed by the general public. Groups may opt to target private sector entities as well.

Activists view the government as the most effective agent of change due to its capacity to implement large-scale policies and regulations. Their efforts are often directed at urging the government to adopt more ambitious climate policies, such as committing to carbon neutrality and investing in renewable energy. However, this reliance on governmental action can potentially foster a dependence on authorities to solve climate issues instead of grassroots solutions.

Beyond governmental engagement, activists also seek to raise awareness and inspire action among the general public, particularly other young people. Public education campaigns, community events, and social media outreach are commonly used to mobilise support and encourage sustainable practices. The SG Climate Rally is one such example of a large mobilisation campaign targeted at the general public.

Beyond the government and general public, youth climate groups may target private sector entities as well. For instance, NTU Divest, a student-led group advocating for divestment from fossil fuels, sees itself as having a "watchdog" role. Formed in 2020, the group engages in dialogue with different offices within NTU to call for more transparent communication about the university's investment, most notably in the fossil fuel industry. In May 2024, NTU Divest protested against a $60 million corporate laboratory partnership between NTU, ExxonMobil, A*Star, and the National Research Foundation, calling for greater clarity on how exactly the partnership would facilitate the transition to clean energy.[6] The group wanted to ensure that the partnership created positive social and environmental benefits and was not merely a greenwashing project.[7] NTU and ExxonMobil responded that the partnership would benefit society, but have not responded directly to the students' desire for more details on the project.[8]

Conclusion

Having outlined the youth climate activism landscape in Singapore, the next part will discuss some challenges and their potential impact on social cohesion.

Endnotes

1. "4 youth panels tasked to find 'hacks' to address life, jobs, tech and environmental concern: NYC", *TODAY*, November 25, 2023. https://www.todayonline.com/singapore/4-youth-panels-tasked-find-hacks-address-life-jobs-tech-and-environmental-concerns-nyc-2311916.
2. K. Han, "Climate change activists test strict Singapore protest law", *Al-Jazeera*, April 10 2020. https://www.aljazeera.com/news/2020/4/10/climate-change-activists-test-strict-singapore-protest-laws.
3. "TODAY youth survey: Climate crisis strikes fear, pessimism but youths believe Govt policies can make the most impact", TODAY, November 4, 2022. https://www.todayonline.com/singapore/today-youth-survey-climate-crisis-fear-pessemism-government-policies-2034066.
4. "Public action", *LepakinSG*. https://lepakinsg.wordpress.com/activities/publicaction/.
5. "Food sustainability", *LepakinSG*. https://lepakinsg.wordpress.com/food-sustainability/.
6. See NTU Divest Instagram page, https://www.instagram.com/p/C63ssbPLAaO/?utm_source=ig_web_copy_link&igsh=MzRlODBiNWFlZA==.
7. *Ibid.*
8. R. Hicks, "Singapore student activists question ExxonMobil backing of low carbon solutions lab", *Eco-Business*, May 17, 2024. https://www.eco-business.com/news/singapore-student-activists-question-exxonmobil-backing-of-low-carbon-solutions-lab/.

CHAPTER 9

Generation Green: How Young Activists are Shaping Singapore's Climate Future Part 2

Amanda Huan

Key Points
- Youth climate activists in Singapore face three major challenges: (a) government engagement, (b) the issue of "ageing out", and (c) challenges in communicating effectively.
- Depending on the sincerity and breadth of government–activist group engagement, the activism could either remain steady or become more assertive.
- To foster a more inclusive and effective climate movement, the government can consider engaging with as many youth groups as possible.
- To help youth climate activists contribute better to policy discussions, the government can also consider increasing its investment in education and capacity-building initiatives for youth climate activists.
- To ensure sustained and meaningful engagement, the government can consider institutionalising youth participation in decision-making processes related to climate and environmental policy.

Introduction

Youth climate activists in Singapore face three major challenges. The first concerns government engagement, the second is the issue of "ageing out", and the third relates to the challenges in communicating effectively.

Government engagement/collaboration

One of the primary challenges faced by youth climate activists in Singapore is deciding whether and how to engage/collaborate with the government. On the one hand, working with the government can provide access to resources, platforms, and influence that can drive substantial policy changes. For instance, Farah Sanwari, co-founder of FiTree, an Islamic environmental group that helps the Muslim community understand environmental issues, was selected to join Minister for Sustainability and the Environment Grace Fu, at the United Nations Voluntary National Review in 2023. While at the UN, Farah was able to leverage the platform to talk about the inclusion of different perspectives for progress to happen on environmental issues.[1]

On the other hand, this engagement can sometimes lead to compromises that may dilute the movement's objectives or create perceptions of co-optation. For instance, Kate Yeo, part of the Singapore Youth for Climate Action (SYCA), a youth climate action group, was cognisant that engaging with the government might inadvertently send a signal of one having been co-opted. She was able to converse with negotiators and people from the Ministry of Sustainability and the Environment and the National Climate Change Secretariat at the COP27 climate talks in Egypt. Speaking on her experiences at COP27, she deliberately chose to use an NGO badge (as opposed to a government badge) as she did not want the affiliation and wanted to be better able to network freely with other delegates.[2]

Balancing the need for cooperation with maintaining an independent, critical stance is a delicate task that continues to shape the strategies and effectiveness of climate activism in the country. To this end, while most youth climate action groups engage in public discussions with government agencies, some youth climate action groups have decidedly opted to use more expressive means. The SG Climate Rally is one such group. The organiser of the first mass climate rally in Singapore in 2019, SG Climate Rally purposefully aims to raise awareness about issues such as climate justice through its "loud" actions (e.g., organised rallies). It hopes that with the large rally turnouts, it can send a signal to the government that climate action is a top concern for members of Singapore society and encourage the government to do more. At its rallies, participants are encouraged to write postcards or emails to their respective MPs (members of parliament). One spokesperson for SG Climate Rally remarked that group members saw themselves fulfilling other roles in the climate advocacy ecosystem: "SG Climate Rally recognises that our place might not always be behind the closed doors of policy discussions or the working groups of think-tanks. Instead, our main role is to try and do the work of organising, directly challenging and transferring the power".[3] While it is difficult to exactly ascertain the group's impact, its attempts at persuading politicians to care more seemed to work; there were more politicians in attendance at the 2023 rally than in 2019.

Ageing out

A second major challenge for youth climate activists is the issue of "ageing out", a significant challenge within the climate activism scene, and not just specific to Singapore. As young activists grow older, they often transition out of direct activism roles due to career, family, and other life commitments. However, this does not necessarily mean they disengage from the cause. Many continue to contribute to sustainability efforts in various capacities, such as through professional roles in environmental organisations, advocacy work, or personal sustainable practices. Youths choose to go into climate activism purposefully; it is not just a fad, and policymakers and society alike would be remiss to think that the wave of youth climate activism will go away like other trends. The "ageing out" phenomenon does highlight the need for continual recruitment and mentorship of new activists to sustain the movement. As a result of this "ageing out" effect, most youth climate action groups tend to rely on a small core group of volunteers and an expanded pool of more ad hoc volunteers to share the heavy workload. Groups typically rely on fresh university entrants for "fresh blood", though some groups have closed down or become defunct when they are unable to find successors.

Communication style

A third major challenge for youth climate activists concerns their communication style. Effective communication is crucial for any social movement, and youth climate activists in Singapore face specific challenges in this area. How messages are framed can significantly impact public perception and support. Missteps in communication can lead to backlash or misunderstandings, undermining the movement's goals. For example, in March 2023, SYCA released an Instagram post which responded to Minister Grace Fu's announcement that Singapore was a potential claimant for Loss and Damage funding. In its post,

SYCA announced that it was "shocked to hear of this development, given that the debate was previously focused on whether Singapore should contribute to the fund. In releasing this public statement, we sincerely hope that the Ministry of Sustainability and the Environment can clarify the statement, and that Singapore will not be a claimant for Loss and Damage funds. As a wealthy nation, the least we can do is to support other developing nations in need of funding, not hinder them".[4] The post was premature, particularly since the government had not yet decided whether it was going to claim from the fund and was stating factually that it qualified as a claimant state.[5] SYCA activists felt that following the incident, they were excluded from government engagement initiatives.[6] Other climate action groups claimed that they were also "sidelined" because they had put out statements that were misaligned with official positions.[7] Continued engagement between the government and youth climate activists can prevent such misunderstandings from occurring and allow for better all-round accountability.

Youth Climate Activism and Social Cohesion

Could youth climate activism impact social cohesion? It depends. The future of youth climate activism in Singapore hinges significantly on government–activist engagement. Depending on the sincerity and breadth of such engagement, the activism could either remain steady or become more assertive.

If the government continues to engage with youth climate activists in a sincere and inclusive manner, it is likely that the activism will remain steady rather than become more aggressive. Singaporean youth are generally pragmatic and recognise the importance of constructive dialogue over disruptive actions. They see little value in "acting out" merely for the sake of it and prefer to work within established systems to achieve their goals. Effective and transparent engagement can channel their energies into productive avenues, reducing the likelihood of confrontational tactics.

However, if the government engages only with selected groups, there is a risk of creating an echo chamber. Selective engagement can alienate a broader spectrum of youth activists and stifle diverse perspectives. This could lead to frustration and a sense of exclusion among those not represented, resulting in a more fragmented and potentially aggressive activism landscape. The concern is that debate and decision-making will become elite-driven, sidelining the voices of genuine grassroots movements and leading to increased dissatisfaction and activism outside the official channels.

Separately, should the government reduce its level of youth engagement, there is a strong possibility that youth climate activism will become more fervent and public. Feeling sidelined or aggrieved, youth activists are likely to demand greater accountability and transparency from the government. This could manifest in more frequent and assertive public actions, such as protests and rallies. Additionally, young activists are increasingly evaluating the environmental policies of different political parties and may express their discontent through the election ballot box. For example, in 2020, SG Climate Rally and Speak for Climate collaborated on GreenWatch, a campaign that assessed the manifestos of the various political parties based on how they addressed aspects of climate change.[8] A decline in government engagement could thus drive a shift towards other forms of advocacy and political expression, including more intense scrutiny of party platforms and voting behaviours influenced by climate concerns.

Policy Recommendations

The climate cause is close to the hearts of youth as they are the ones who will face the dire consequences. As outlined on the United Nations website, "Young people's unprecedented mobilisation around the world shows the massive power they possess to hold decision-makers accountable. Their message is clear: the older generation has failed, and it is the young who will pay in full – with their very futures".[9] Youth climate activism is key in galvanising support among communities to take greater and quicker action to address climate change. The following are some policy recommendations for decision-makers to consider as the youth climate activism scene in Singapore continues to evolve.

First, to foster a more inclusive and effective climate movement, the government can consider engaging with as many youth groups as possible. Engaging effectively with youth requires a deep understanding of their perspectives and motivations. Young activists are still learning the nuances of communication and advocacy, and their boldness and passion can sometimes lead to missteps. The government should approach these interactions with patience and empathy, recognising that mistakes are part of the learning process. By fostering an environment where youth feel heard and supported, even when they make errors, the government can help cultivate a more resilient and informed activist community and provide guidance and support. This approach acknowledges the learning curve inherent in activism and encourages continued participation and growth.

Second, to help youth climate activists contribute better to policy discussions, the government can also consider increasing its investment in education and capacity-building initiatives for youth climate activists. This includes workshops on policy development, public speaking, and strategic communication, as well as access to resources and mentorship from experienced activists and professionals in the field. The government can also consider incorporating climate activism into the education curriculum to promote classroom discussions on environmental problems. The #GreenHacks youth panel initiative mentioned in the previous chapter is a step in the right direction. As part of the initiative, youths will participate in workshops aimed at equipping them with a better understanding of the policymaking process. By providing them with knowledge of the policymaking process, youth climate activists will be able to offer more nuanced and informed feedback on the government's environmental policies and initiatives.

Third, to ensure sustained and meaningful engagement, the government can consider institutionalising youth participation in decision-making processes related to climate and environmental policy. This can be achieved by creating advisory councils or committees that include youth representatives, ensuring their voices are heard at all levels of policy development. The formation of Youth Circles by the Ministry of Culture, Community and Youth to address specific policy issues such as food waste is one way in which the government started to partner with the youth in policymaking.[10] Initiatives such as the Youth Circles and the more recent Youth Panels, however, are often on a small scale and discussions are conducted with a small (and often regular) group of individuals. The government should consider other feedback mechanisms and platforms for dialogue to maintain a dynamic and responsive engagement between youth activists and policymakers.

Conclusion

In conclusion, youth climate activism in Singapore is driven by a deep-seated concern for the future, a desire to address perceived inaction, and a commitment to making a substantial impact. As the movement continues to evolve, both the government and youth climate activist groups alike should do more to foster a constructive and dynamic relationship. This collaborative approach is essential for addressing the complex and urgent challenges posed by climate change, paving the way for a sustainable and resilient future for Singapore.

Endnotes

1. "Singapore to emphasise the role youths play in driving climate action as Grace Fu visits UN next week", *CNA*, July 14, 2023. https://www.channelnewsasia.com/singapore/sustainability-development-goals-un-singapore-voluntary-national-review-youths-3629206.
2. R. Hicks, "'You cannot be an activist and not put yourself at risk': Singapore climate campaigner Kate Yeo", *Eco-Business*, April 11, 2023. https://www.eco-business.com/news/you-cannot-be-an-activist-and-not-put-yourself-at-risk-singapore-climate-campaigner-kate-yeo/.
3. J. Ho, "Climate change is a bread-and-butter issue: SG climate rally organiser", *The Edge*, July 11, 2024. https://www.theedgesingapore.com/news/climate-change/climate-change-bread-and-butter-issue-sg-climate-rally-organiser.
4. See Singapore Youth for Climate Action Instagram post. https://www.instagram.com/p/CptwjTzShim/?utm_source=ig_web_copy_link&igsh=MzRlODBiNWFlZA==.
5. Singapore subsequently announced that it would not claim from the fund and would instead help other countries access the funding. See "Singapore won't claim from climate loss & damage fund; will help other countries access money from it: Grace Fu", *The Business Times*, December 11, 2023. https://www.businesstimes.com.sg/esg/singapore-wont-claim-climate-loss-damage-fund-will-help-other-countries-access-money-it-grace.
6. This was communicated to me by various youth climate activists who were familiar with the incident.
7. *Ibid.*
8. "Greenwatch", *SG Climate Rally*, 2023. https://www.sgclimaterally.com/greenwatch. See the resulting scorecard here: http://scorecard.sgclimaterally.com/.
9. "Youth in action", *United Nations Climate Action*. https://www.un.org/en/climatechange/youth-in-action.
10. "Partnering the young and the not so old", Speech by Mr Alvin Tan, Minister of State for Culture, Community and Youth & Trade and Industry at the Committee of Supply Debate 2021. https://www.mccy.gov.sg/about-us/news-and-resources/speeches/2021/mar/partnering-the-young-and-the-not-so-old.

PART 5
FOSTERING SOCIAL COHESION

CHAPTER 10

Identity, Youth, and Activism in the Diaspora – The British Sikh Community

Jasvir Singh

Key Points
- The Khalistan movement appears to be highly appealing to Sikhs born after 1984, whereas the older generations do not consider it to be a priority issue.
- Several events involving Sikhs have transformed perceptions of threats into tangible fears.
- There is an evident need to develop spaces for discourse regarding political awareness and activism when it comes to Gen Z and Millennial Sikhs.
- Creating a safe space for such discussions allows views to be aired without a sense of disenfranchisement or discontentment.
- Gurdwaras also have a role to play here.

Introduction

The Sikh communities outside of India have experienced great change over the last few years, with a growing sense of confidence, particularly within the English-speaking world. Some of this is a result of 2nd-, 3rd-, and 4th-generation Sikhs, who have been born and brought up in diasporic communities across the world and who are more secure in their own identities than perhaps the 1st-generation Sikhs were, namely those who had travelled from abroad as pioneers to make homes in countries they were not born in.

In the UK in particular, the number of Sikh MPs in the British Parliament has increased fivefold from 2 to 11 in the July 2024 general election.[1] The impact of such a seismic shift in political representation cannot be underestimated, especially considering that the British Sikh community is only half a million strong. By way of comparison, there are believed to be about 13 MPs of Sikh heritage in India, which has a Sikh population of 22 million.[2]

Differences within the Community

Against the backdrop of a rise in confidence, we have also seen the emergence of differences within the Sikh communities, as well as issues which are specifically affecting the Sikh communities rather than wider society and which highlight societal and communal differences.

One of the clearest examples of intra-community issues is the intergenerational differences between 1st-generation Sikhs and those who have been born in the diasporic country. Cultural clashes can emerge between the various generations about how institutions within the communities should be run or where the focus is when it comes to investing in the future of those communities.

The Sikh community in Crawley, West Sussex, until recently had a single gurdwara (Sikh place of worship). The charity owning the gurdwara purchased a much larger site nearby which was developed into a new gurdwara. Whilst the majority of the sangat (congregation) has moved to the new site, some have decided to remain at the old site and continue operating the gurdwara there. The gurdwara at the old site appears to be run primarily for the benefit of Sikhs who have recently arrived in the UK,[3] whilst the gurdwara at the new site is being run primarily by Sikhs who arrived decades ago alongside those who were born and brought up in the UK.[4] Although the charity running the new site has legal ownership of the old site, the sangat at the old site has so far refused to move out and allow the old site to be sold. It is a fascinating microcosm of the issues of a culture clash.

Sikh Political Awareness and the Khalistan Movement

Sikh theology emphasises the need to strike a balance between the socio-political/temporal and the spiritual aspects of one's life, otherwise known as the concept of Miri-Piri.[5] It can find itself manifested in political awareness and discourse. It is worth bearing in mind that the Sikh faith developed into a politically aware movement in 17th-century India as a means of challenging the Mughal empire, particularly when it was seen to be authoritarian in manner.

The concept of Miri-Piri can be found in the present day through Sikh political activism and movements. Due to its origins, it can often take an anti-authoritarian stance and have an iconoclastic element to it. Recent examples of this include the Khalistan movement, the Farmers' Protests in India, and other international causes involving groups perceived to be oppressed.

The Khalistan movement is focussed on the demand for a separate Sikh state to be carved out of the Indian state of Punjab. The Indian Government finds this a grave threat to its stability because the secession of any of its states could find the entire federal system unravelling. The demand for Khalistan is also closely entwined with the events of 1984 in India, including the storming of the Golden Temple complex in Amritsar by the Indian Army in June 1984, as well as the genocidal riots against Sikhs in November 1984 following the PM Indira Gandhi's assassination by her bodyguards who were Sikh.[6]

The Khalistan Movement, Activism, and the Younger Generation of Sikhs

The Khalistan movement appears to be highly appealing to Sikhs born after 1984, whereas the older generations do not consider it to be a priority issue. The findings of the British Sikh Report 2023[7] reported that when respondents were asked "*What are the top three priorities for the Indian state of Punjab?*", 16% of them said they viewed independence/sovereignty as one of those top three priorities, arguably showing their support for Khalistan. This was made up of 24% of those aged 19 or less, and 19% of those aged 20–34. However, only 9% of those aged 65–79 and only 2% of those aged 80 or over saw it as a top three priority.[8]

Part of this is likely to be due to the passing of time. Sikhs who lived through the events of 1984 were deeply traumatised by the impact, especially as there were still very strong connections with family members in India. The media blackout for several days in early June 1984 meant that there was no way of knowing whether family members were dead or alive and journalists were banned from travelling to Punjab to report on the extent of the Indian Army's operations there. The militancy period in Punjab in the 1980s and early 1990s was extremely destabilising, both economically and psychologically, and the majority of Sikhs who remember it simply do not want to revisit that period of history again.

Now that we are four decades on, younger generations do not have those living memories. For them, the focus is on how the concept of Khalistan would fit into the modern world, the importance of autonomous existence and self-determination which is in tune with Sikh theology, achieving justice for the victims of 1984, and the perceived discrimination against Sikhs and the spotlight on anti-Sikh activities in present-day India.

These generational differences can generally be best described as being between those who want to create a utopian state for Sikhs in the 21st century and those who remember the horrors of 1984 and the militancy in Punjab and do not want to go through that pain again.

Social and niche community media have also a role to play here. Since the mid-2010s, attacks within India on Sikhs, gurdwaras, or the Sikh scriptures have become important issues within the wider Sikh community because of the way those stories have been circulated via social media. Even though such attacks are very rare, they became a prominent news story for Sikhs which were first circulated on social media such as Twitter (now X), Instagram and Tik Tok, shared via WhatsApp and Snapchat, and then broadcast by Sikh outlets on YouTube and on satellite TV stations.

The rise in such stories, which would previously have not had such prominence and perhaps would not have even been reported in print or broadcast media, creates the impression of Sikhs being under constant attack in India. This gives further impetus to the perceived need for a separate Sikh state, particularly when it comes to younger generations.

However, certain events can also lead such perceptions of threats to become tangible fears. In September 2023, Canadian PM Justin Trudeau accused India of involvement in the killing of a prominent

Canadian Sikh Khalistani, Hardeep Singh Nijjar.[9] Since then, concerns have grown about the Indian Government and its response towards Khalistanis, with some Khalistani Sikhs becoming afraid of being targeted. This has led to wider anxiety amongst younger Sikhs, in particular about what they view as politically motivated killings, regardless of their own views on Khalistan, as well as amongst much older Sikhs who have sought political asylum in the diaspora due to their Khalistani activism or support.[10]

The more recent concerns about the Indian Government came soon after the Farmers' Protests in 2020/2021, where Sikhs were seen to be the main victims of the State. The Farmers' Protests took place during the COVID-19 pandemic when social media usage was extremely high in the UK[11] and information regarding the protestors was being circulated on non-traditional media. This created the impression of mainstream media not being interested in the Farmers' Protests and lending a conspiracy theory element to the worries amongst many Sikhs. However, this was compounded by a BBC News report in November 2021 which stated that fake social media posts about the Farmers' Protests were promoting divisive narratives.[12]

Since the October 7, 2023 attacks by Hamas on Israel, and the subsequent Israel/Gaza war, there has been support from some within the Sikh community in the English-speaking world for Palestine and Gaza. Again, much of this is being led by younger diaspora-born Sikhs who view the persecution of Palestinians as being a cause to rally around and provide support for, particularly in light of the Sikh concept of supporting the most vulnerable and downtrodden in society. This is one example of alignment with international causes that go beyond the Sikh community itself.

Conclusion: Engaging Gen Z and Millennial Sikhs

There is an evident need to develop spaces for discourse regarding political awareness and activism when it comes to Gen Z and Millennial Sikhs. Creating a safe space for such discussions allows views to be aired without a sense of disenfranchisement or discontentment. Listening circles[13] are a good way of creating such a space and they also allow the root causes of discontentment to be explored. During the far-right riots in Britain in August 2024, listening circles were used by Sikh and South Asian organisations so that people could talk about how they were feeling and gain emotional support through it.[14]

Context and understanding are important when looking at grievances from members or sections of the Sikh communities. Without context, there is a risk of misunderstanding why the grievance is being raised or discussed in the first place. For example, the reason why there was global Sikh support for the Farmers' Protests was because the majority of farmers protesting had come from Punjab, where agriculture has been a mainstay of the economy for generations, and because many diasporic Sikhs have links to ancestral farmland still held by family members in Punjab today.

Gurdwaras also have a role to play here. There is an evident need to adapt to the challenges of the modern day and to use the younger members of the sangat to help with that. Having youth officers on the executive committees in gurdwaras, as well as youth boards, will ensure that they have a vested interest in their places of worship and the institutions of their faith. Having lectures in English, film showings, youth-based festivals, sporting events, and other such activities will create a space that is welcoming and supportive for the changing needs of Sikhs, as well as bringing the generations together as a community.

Endnotes

1. "Record Number of Sikh MPs in Parliament after General Election", *BBC News*, July 11, 2024, https://www.bbc.co.uk/news/articles/clkyx3y1yjno.
2. "Sikhs and Hindus at the Crossroads", *Times of India Blog*, November 23, 2019, https://timesofindia.indiatimes.com/blogs/mind-the-gap/sikhs-and-hindus-at-the-crossroads/.
3. Crawley Gurdwara Instagram page, 2020, https://www.instagram.com/gurdwara_crawley/.
4. Sri Guru Singh Sabha Gurdwara Crawley Instagram page, 2020. https://www.instagram.com/srigurusinghsabha_crawley/.
5. "Miri Piri", in SikhiWiki. https://www.sikhiwiki.org/index.php/Miri_Piri.
6. P. Singh, *1984: India's Guilty Secret* (New Delhi: Rupa Publications India, 2017).
7. The British Sikh Report seeks to identify the needs and wants of the Sikh population in the UK. The annual report forms the basis for engagement with political and community leaders and helps inspire others to help run and create initiatives to cater to Sikhs in Britain. See British Sikh Report website. https://britishsikhreport.org/.
8. J. Singh, *Review of British Sikh Report 2023*, J. Virdee (ed.). https://britishsikhreport.org/wp-content/uploads/2024/01/British-Sikh-Report-2023.pdf.
9. "Hardeep Singh Nijjar: Canada accuses India of role in Sikh leader's murder", *BBC News*, September 18, 2023. https://www.bbc.co.uk/news/uk-66848041.
10. "Death, suspicion and the Sikh Diaspora", *BBC Radio 4*. https://www.bbc.co.uk/programmes/m001xp5w.
11. "Adults' media use and attitudes", *Ofcom*, September 27, 2023. https://www.ofcom.org.uk/media-use-and-attitudes/media-habits-adults/adults-media-use-and-attitudes/.
12. "Farm laws: Sikhs being targeted by fake social media profiles", *BBC News*, November 24, 2021. https://www.bbc.co.uk/news/world-asia-india-59338245.
13. "Listening circles are a specific type of circle designed to help people process an event or issue that poses a challenge or harm to their communities or has impacted people in a significant way. They are voluntary, community-oriented forums aimed at providing an equitable opportunity for all attendees to have voice. Listening circles can be used in a variety of settings, including communities, workplaces, schools, organisations, neighbourhoods, universities, and within families". See "Facilitating Listening Circles", *International Institute for Restorative Practices*. https://www.iirp.edu/professional-development/facilitating-listening-circles#:~:text=Listening%20circles%20are%20a%20specific,all%20attendees%20to%20have%20voice.
14. South Asian Heritage Month (SAHM) Instagram page. https://www.instagram.com/p/C-TJlwZqTYg.

© 2025 Nanyang Technological University
https://doi.org/10.1142/9789819812691_0011

CHAPTER 11

Fostering Social Cohesion by Tackling Shared Challenges as "We"

Amanda Huan and Leong Chan-Hoong

Key Points
- Social cohesion is crucial to maintain peace, stability and inclusion.
- Fostering cohesion can be achieved through the emphasis on common immutable identities such as ethnicity, religion, and lineage, or through shared experiences, especially in tackling common challenges that affect all communities.
- While much research has been done in the former, the benefits of shared pain points are less recognised.
- There is potential to leverage on shared challenges to bridge tribal differences and forge a common goal for all.

Introduction

On 29 July 2024, three young girls were fatally stabbed and many more seriously injured in the seaside town of Southport in the United Kingdom. Rumours that the murderer was a Muslim immigrant triggered nationwide anti-Islam and anti-immigrant riots, instigated by supporters of the far right as they stirred up primordial instincts along religious and racial lines by seeding the sense of injustice and hatred between communities.

The unrest led to hundreds of arrests and severely undermined the social fabric of the country. The carnage was all but a solemn reminder to Singaporeans about the importance of cohesion in multicultural societies – it is a form of "invisible glue" that binds a united people, both in peacetime and during crises.

Divisions Within and Beyond Our Borders

While diversity has enriched our heritage, the prospects of identity-based conflicts remain a possibility.

Tensions along tribal identities can be sparked by events within and beyond national borders, amplified by the dissemination of fake news and social media's echo chamber effect. The riots in the UK may have a domestic genesis, but the fault lines can also be exploited by state-sponsored actors to subvert the country's stability, preying on internal rivalries and community chasms.

Deploying these strategies to provoke perceived existential threats is not novel, and Singapore is not immune against such designs.

Colonial powers had in the past incited divisions in their occupied settlements. The ancient Romans are known for their *divide et impera* (divide and conquer) strategy where they sought separate alliances with each occupied village, pitching one community against another and maintaining tension between the groups so that the Romans could continue to govern.

In recent years, global events such as the conflict between Russia and Ukraine, the Gaza crisis, and the ongoing contest between the US and China have encouraged each side to sow civic discord as a weapon against its adversary.

Taking Stock of Our Strategies to Foster Cohesion

Notwithstanding our internal primordial instincts and the external forces that seek to divide societies, Singaporeans are generally cognisant of our fragility on existing fault lines. As Senior Minister Lee Hsien Loong alluded to in a recent interview, building trust, confidence, and reciprocity between tribal communities is always a work in progress.

How might tribalism be overcome? The schism can be bridged in a number of ways. Here, we highlight two approaches towards fostering cohesion.

First, societies may identify a common heritage and a disposition to forge psychological ties. This includes but is not limited to shared values, social norms, or spoken language. This type of national identity is percolated and strengthened mostly through formal and structured institutions such as education, legislation, and law enforcement.

For instance, the creation of the Singapore National Pledge was intended to inculcate national consciousness in the young nation. By highlighting the commitment of Singaporeans to shared values like justice and equality, the National Pledge sought to imbue its citizens with a sense of national pride and patriotism.

The second and perhaps less familiar strategy is grounded in the principle of shared predicament, such as the collective effort in tackling common challenges. This approach is more organic and it transcends tribal boundaries. One example is volunteer firefighters in Australia, a country that is prone to bushfires. According to 2022 national figures in Australia, there are about 190,000 volunteers working alongside 20,000 paid professional staff, representing about 0.8% of the total Australian population. This public institution paved the way for a uniquely Australian experience that many respect no matter their background.

Uncovering the Hidden Intersections in Our Daily Lives

National identity and cohesion are amorphous concepts. We do not carry with us the definitions of unity and citizenship in our daily routines, even though we may understand the potential harm arising from conflicts such as those along religious and racial contours.

As Singapore society matures, our lifestyles have grown more complex with fewer intersections across diverse communities. We need to revisit how social cohesion can be fostered, specifically how to harness social rituals and challenges that we can all resonate with in building the "invisible glue".

Importantly, we can appreciate how the process can bring us together as a community, even though these experiences are not always favourable.

For instance, many Singaporean men recall their time in the National Service, a significant rite of passage, with nostalgia, even though the two years of regimental training are both physically and psychologically imposing.

Similarly, Singaporeans who have gone through the local education system will remember their formative years in school. While the national examinations in primary and secondary school can be stressful, the friendships forged over core curriculum activities, make-up lessons, and study groups remain a part of their collective memory in adulthood. These bonds often transcend religious and racial boundaries and are cornerstones of camaraderie and belongingness, just like the National Service.

Beyond these normative rituals, we also share much in common in tackling national crises. According to a study in 2016, Singaporeans rated the SARS (2003)[1] pandemic as the most important event in the city-state's modern history as it was the most emotionally relatable event, regardless of one's socio-economic background.

Collectively, developmental milestones and crises have made us stronger as one people.

It demands that we look past our differences to address immediate or future crises, and in doing so, foster a shared understanding as one people.

Research has found that collective challenges, not just triumphs and successes, catalyse strong bonding among members of a community.

Indeed, to quote American writer Sherrilyn Kenyon, "The strongest steel is forged by the fires of hell".

Conclusion

To date, we have traditionally viewed cohesion in celebratory terms as we commemorate important events such as National Day. If we focus solely on our common heritage or "feel-good" community festivals to forge psychological ties, we will miss out on the other opportunities to nurture cohesion through organic journeys.

Singapore has achieved much progress in identifying and forging its national culture, such as its core values, commitment to meritocracy, and multicultural practices. We have established a distinctive identity and are proud of our ubiquitous traits such as the use of Singlish, indulgence in good food, and a progressive attitude towards governance and community development.

Beyond these attributes, we can further highlight our shared experiences in coping with challenges, big or small and explore indigenous ways to recognise the everyday rites of passage. For instance, could SAFRA or other community bodies provide discounted rates on venues for servicemen reunions? Could the education ministry offer financial and non-financial support for neighbourhood schools to help foster more active alumni participation? Could we have a local "Remembrance Day" to show appreciation for our fallen comrades in the healthcare sector?

Social cohesion is shaped by a multitude of experiences, both pleasant and unpleasant. Forging meaningful ties with people from diverse communities can be built on shared experiences in overcoming common challenges, even if these experiences are painful to all.

Endnote

1. C. H. Leong, M. Choo, E. Ho, V. Lim, P. Seah, and W. W. Yang, "Study on the perceptions of Singapore's history", in C. Soon and S. F. Hoe (eds.) *Singapore Perspectives 2015* (Singapore: World Scientific, 2016), pp. 153–187.

www.ingramcontent.com/pod-product-compliance
Lightning Source LLC
Chambersburg PA
CBHW070839150625
27790CB00017B/16